# Three Governing Laws in Genesis and Romans

by Dr. Solomon Chijindu Okpali

DORRANCE PUBLISHING CO
EST. 1920
PITTSBURGH, PENNSYLVANIA 15238

Dorrance Publishing Co
585 Alpha Drive
Suite 103
Pittsburgh, PA 15238
Visit our website at www.dorrancebookstore.com

ISBN: 979-8-8868-3213-6
eISBN: 979-8-8868-3786-5

# CONTENTS

I dedicate this piece to all teachers and faithful followers
of the word who will tarry to the end.

# ACKNOWLEDGMENTS

All glory belongs to God Almighty and the Author and finisher of my faith, Jesus Christ.

Identifying the eternal Laws addressed in this piece took me through the Word and several references and books authored by distinguished men of God. These authors and their work include Smith's Bible Dictionary, Jimmy Swaggart's, The Sin Nature, The Seventh Chapter of Romans, and The Law of the Spirit. Frank Stagg's New Testament Theology, and Easton's Law of Moses. Other works include Charles Hodges' Quoted by grace to you and Borgman Paul's, David, Saul, and God; Gerhard Von Rad's Old Testament Theology (Vol. 1&11); Kugel James' Tradition of the Bible, and Strong's Concordance of the Bible.

To these authors, thank you for your work for the kingdom's cause and especially for providing the knowledge base for this piece.

And I will always be grateful to my children for their continuing moral and emotional support. Their innocent presence drives the focus in me, always.

Solomon Chijindu Okpali, P.HD.

# INTRODUCTION

From the very beginning, the man walked himself unto destruction from the comfort of his finite wisdom. Although the acceptance that Satan's deception has a pivotal role in the man's recklessness towards God's Law is catholic, it is arguable that man's self-will and pride were more accelerative to his submissiveness to the Serpent's enteritis than the Satanic lure itself. In the same vein, Eve may have presented herself as a ready tool of the evil one in the trap of Humankind to death. Still, it is equally agreeable that Adam was supposed to possess superior intelligence, and therefore, more equipped to discern truth from lies.

Again, Adam stood tall at the apex of creation and directly received the commandments from Yahweh. Biblical evidence insists, therefore, that Adam failed. He chose lies and the love of his woman, who was "bone of his bone and flesh of his flesh" (Gen. 2:23). The effect was instantaneous. He fell from abundance to nothingness and died in his flesh.

This first act of disobedience incurred the invitation of death for humanity, precisely as God had pre-warned. Apart from its result in the loss of God's glory, sin also gave birth to other things: self-will, self-effort, struggle, and exploitation of carnal intelligence, all of which are filth even before the shadow of the Almighty. It is also remarkable that the LORD God shed Man's innocence immediately at this point. For the first time, the man realized the essence of his nature hitherto outside his emotional reality: Nakedness. He lost forever innocence, which was the clothing of his divine nature.

Soon, man would lose the abundance of the Garden and the security and love empowered by God. He would forgo this peace not precisely because he disobeyed God by eating the forbidden fruit, but essentially because he chose the words of other beings when faced with a choice involving God's will. He tacitly recognised the Serpent's instructions and respected the adoring words of his wife at the expense of God's command.

However, in this subdued state of expectations, man rose in pride, and instead of honoring repentance tapped his carnal intelligence and finite wisdom. He wove for himself intriguing clothing from fig leaves and went into hiding. Nevertheless, of course, this covering from man's hand-made materials presented in vivid inadequacies. It revealed the incompleteness of his self-will while taking actions and embarking on unguided endeavors, especially in matters concerning relationships with his maker. Adam did not see it or could not see it, and it stays on to this day.

Sin, thus, separated man from his God. And so, he found himself alone in nakedness because he chose to struggle for his livelihood. From this point onward, his efforts in life would recapture the lost essence and unity with God. The zeal for unity with God then became the core of his existence. The Omniscient knows that His creation would continue the dive unto foolishness. Being Love and Benevolence, He Created a standard for growth, righteousness, and deliverance.

However, there must be a nucleus, a people, through which the seed would soothe to manifest the divine will. In no time, He chose a people who became His people. He would teach humanity His principles through His people. Meanwhile, he sowed a seed that transpired in Abraham and lived on to Isaac, down to Jacob, and thence

Israel. Israel grew in population as the earth multiplied dimensionally but with SIN's unrivaled essence.

Using the Prophets, God made His will known to man. He would administer correction through these same chosen people when an error occurred and redirect the people back to Him. Thus, the Law for humanity was in place, and guidance was not lacking. Nevertheless, it was evident that the Law's implementation proved insufficient to control the wild in the flesh. Thus, despite the Law's good intentions and directions, its workings proved inadequate to lead man to God.

Still, the Law continued to demonstrate its leadership qualities over time in the chosen people's lives. Apart from its primary role of leading humanity to God, it routinely revealed to man his natural incapability over sin. However, the people repeatedly proved that they remain in their limited mental power to understand the truth about themselves and the essence of the Law.

Sin multiplied, and death reigned. Sacrifices and a series of atonements became unavoidable to clean man of sin and prevail on death. With time, the blood of the sacrificed animals became filthy in the eyes of God. Animal blood was impure and inadequate for cleansing and atonement of sin in the presence of God. It could not meet the standard that had remained in place for the Lamb of the world. This Lamb will, for once, take away the sins of the world and reestablish man's oneness with God. Without this unity with the Creator of the universe, the people will exist in emptiness.

For this cause came Jesus. He was the Lamb. With Jesus came the message of hope he delivered with instructions, as he fulfilled the Law without guilt. With Christ also came the Calvary experience and the sequential work on the cross. At the cross, Jesus perfected the ever-elusive atonement. Here, he established redemption and sealed justification. What once lived as a mirage now became a reality. He now frees Humankind from the entanglement of the overpowering Law and the stings of death.

With the thunderous tearing of the blocked passage into the Holy of Holies at the instance of the Law, man can now walk directly to God through the great High Priest, Jesus Christ. "Seeing then that we have a great high priest that is passed into heavens, Jesus the Son of God." (Heb.4:14). This experience brought a new horizon caped with the institution of a new law, the Law of Love.

The infinite mind is God. Before now, He had chosen among men of twelve special people, the apostles. He sowed seeds in their fertile minds through which he would replenish the world with the new order. As the High Priest gloriously sat at the right hand of God, it became the mission of the twelve to reveal to the people the meaning of the cross of Christ. Their ministries revolved around this fact, and their deaths were unto this cross.

Nevertheless, Jesus came and died that we might live in him unto God. Any man who believes in this truth becomes "a peculiar people" and "a chosen generation."

Against this background, this book will examine the "Fall of Man," "The Laws of Moses," "The Law of Sin and Death," the "Law of the Spirit of Life in Christ Jesus," and other non-less Principles identifiable in the scripture for the good of man.

# CHAPTER ONE

## The Fall of Man

Humankind embeds the original sin consequent of the disobedience of humanity's first parents. The creation of man and the subsequent divine provision of a garden of abode, Eden, necessitated the institution of a bit of control mechanism, testing, and principles of partnership, the adherence of which would sustain the benevolence. It stands against absurdity to emphasize that no such guide existed before creation. After creation, man, having been endowed with authority over all other creatures (Gen. 1:28-30), lived in a Garden without lack. God provided gold and irrigated the land to enhance fertile soil for cultivation. This provision was made without human hands but by God Himself.

In addition to the providence, He blessed man with a soul that was free from the burden of sin:

"And they were both naked, the man and his wife, and were not ashamed" (Gen. 2:25). Original sin as a concept has been a subject of scholarly debate in which each camp or individual attempts to ascribe a standard theological meaning to it. While some scholars see it as a composite moral corruption passed down from Adam through generations of descendants, others attempt to explain it as merely

Adamic fallen nature passed down through his descendants (1). The latter, as applied, seems to have sympathy with the biblical provision:

"Wherefore, as by one man sin entered into the world, and death by sin; and so, death passed upon all men, for that all have sinned" (Rom. 5:12). However, it is of interest that others reject the stance that the "Guilt of the Original Sin" passed down through generations on an equally instructive biblical provision:

"The soul that sins, it shall die. The son shall not bear the iniquity of the father; neither shall the father bear the iniquity of the son: the righteousness of the righteous shall be upon him, and the wickedness of the wicked shall be upon him" (Eze. 18:20). This provision appeals to one's perception as a very empowering theological tool because it suggests that salvation is subjective and personal. However, the consensus seems to accept that the Original Sin is closely related to the Fall of man. However, although "man" refers to humanity, we should remember that "man" as applied may also suggest the first man ever created and through whom the Almighty replenished the earth (Gen. 1:28).

In all, the "Fall of Man" expresses the resentful revolt of Adam and Eve from the Lord God and the consequence of sin bestowed on their posterity (2). Original sin did not seem to involve physical corruption. The first parents did not kill or rub, nor did they main or destroy. Instead, its temperament appears to be an internal weakness in making a divine choice. We can describe it then as either spiritual or ethical disobedience against the Creator.

Still of interest is the varied appraisal of the influence of Adamic nature on humanity. While some Theologians express that humanity naturally inherited corruption from Adam, others seem to believe that Humankind is present in a consistent state with Adam's condition before the Fall (3). Regardless of the divergent views, what seems nourishing is the view that stays consistent with the scripture, especially as it relates to the nature of Adam and his wife after creation. The evident shift from this original state of consciousness to something else after the disobedience becomes the core of the matter. "And they were both naked, the man (Adam) and his wife, and were not ashamed" (Gen. 2:25). Nakedness would suggest the absence of clothing. Not being ashamed of bareness for a man and a woman living together appears to present a human nature not found in today's man.

This view agrees with Satan's insistent that their eyes would open, enabling them to comprehend certain truths that hide outside their consciousness, signifying innocence:

"And the serpent said unto the woman, you shall not surely die for God does know that in the day you eat thereof, then your eyes shall be opened, and you shall be as gods, knowing good and evil" (Gen. 3:5).

Again, Smith's name dictionary explains that "Adam" is "Adamah" for Hebrew and means "Red Earth" from which God formed him; reminding us that Adam was a crowning act of creation — "A perfect man in body and spirit, but as innocent and completely inexperienced as a child." (4) It would seem then that the overriding human attribute that he shed at the Fall was innocence in exchange for the remorseful shame which has remained part of the burden of sin. This absence of divine purity earned man outright expulsion from the garden of Eden. In His Omniscient, the Lord God knew that man in his compromised state would dare the fruit of the Tree of Life:

"And the Lord God said, Behold the man is become as one of us, to know good and evil and now lest he put forth his hands, and take also of the Tree of Life, and eat, and live forever" (Gen. 3:22).

Therefore, in the Fall, the man was inclusively different from his former self. However, this stance denies that the prohibition imposed on Adam regarding "the tree of the knowledge of good and evil" was a test of obedience and responsibility. Thus, the conclusion only attempts to show that man was different at the beginning from what he had become. Therefore, if it is undisputed that Adam was the first parent, we must accept that what he bequeathed to his descendants must be consistent with his nature after his Fall. Then, what humanity inherited from him would be a composite of the Adamic covenant.

Nevertheless, we must recognize an established condition and a "Given Instruction" before Adam's crowning disobedience and reckless exhibition of pride. Here, we find the interplay of the rude characteristics of Law in full swing. Law enhances lawlessness. Without an enactment, the latter is nonexistent. In other words, with a given code, obedience and disobedience become living phenomena. This sequence is unavoidable because it is either one or the other. Nevertheless, in the blissful and bountiful garden in which Adam lived, a law came to taint their environment; the instruction was clear and direct, but it was a law:

"And the LORD God commanded the man, saying, of every tree of the Garden you may freely eat. But of the tree of the knowledge of Good and Evil, you shall not eat of it." (Gen.2:16-17a).

However, without due diligence, they broke this Law and disobedience occurred. The sole duty of the man was to "Dress and keep" this garden (2:15). Still, he had to exercise the responsibility within the confines of this command— a command that came with an appendage of judgment (2:17b), separation from God. "For in the day that thou eatest thereof thou shall die." The "knowledge of Good and Evil" also presents some points of interest. Jehovah Elohim, by his very nature, is everything good. He is love divine. It is inversely proportional to the goodness of God to suggest that He did not expect a man to rival His nature by acquiring these truths. That would amount to evil, but the LORD God hates evil. What appears sympathetic with logic is that He did not qualify man dimensionally suitable to acquire such knowledge at his will. It just could not be through the man's way. Such truths we reach through the order of things, God's way, and by faith in Christ Jesus as humanity would eventually find out. Nevertheless, He bestowed on the man His attributes, for He created him in His image (Gen.1:27). In this experience, we notice the biggest lie of all time. Satan exhibits his mastery in deception and counters God's instruction to Adam by evaluating the substance of the words and with a promise of that which he could not give, making them gods. He guaranteed Eve that she would not die (3:4) and went ahead to expand his lies that God knew their eyes would open and they would become the likeness of gods, knowing good and evil. So, Satan is a liar who promised what he could not give and whose whole existence revolves around deceptions. Therefore, anyone who lusts after Satan becomes a child of the devil, says Jesus:

"You are of your father the devil, and the lust of your father you will do... When he speaks a lie, he speaks of his own: for he is a liar and the father of it." (Jn.8:44)

This reference summarizes the devil's total being, which he passed down to his adherents and those not of God. This ascription to undiscerning Jews, and by implication, all those who oppose God's will, seems apt. One cannot be not a liar while opposing God's will and claiming to be of God. Nevertheless, we have no proof to determine whether Eve acted in omission and commission error or whether her utterances were sequential to her reckless disbelief of God's Word. No matter, it is evident that her response to the Serpent's query presents some additions to the Word of God. Now compare "Gen. 2:16-17" with "Gen.3:3." We cannot posit whether this was a challenge of God's authority. Neither can we ascertain that she might have uttered such words out of innocent excitement elicited by the lure of the Serpent. Humanity's fragile experience with God insists that additions or subtractions from God's Word demonstrate no more minor sin but constitute an irrevocable source of grief. Thus, in the desert discourse, Moses taught the Israelites not to add to the word of God or take anything out of it. In this state of obedience, they would be able to observe and keep the directives to the letter (Deut.4:2).

Instructively, the spontaneous reaction of Adam and Eve at the instant of their disobedience portrays the fact that the physical nature of what man has become could not have been what man was at creation. They may have vibrated at a different level of spiritual frequency and therefore knew no shame. Elsewhere, Jimmy Swaggart has pointed out that man at creation was "Enswathed in ethereal and transfiguring light." This spiritual presentation was man's nature, the divine state of innocence. That shame suddenly became a member of their social experience in their limited numeric number suggests that something gave way to something—which transformed their satiated state of living to yearn for wants and needs. In sequence, they ate the forbidden fruit, became aware of their nakedness, made an apron of fig leaves for clothing, and, above all foolishness, hid from God. The man had fallen. It occurred by the lust of the eyes and flesh, compounded by pride. The innocence was lost, the likeness of God dimmed, and the purity which clothed their bodies vanished.

It is appropriate to observe that when the Lord God laid down the command of the forbidden fruit before Adam, He had not created Eve, and she was not in the picture. It would seem then that her limited understanding of God's Word may have aided her lustful bent to the push of the subtle Serpent. Whatever the reason for such rebellion may be, the result was reactions in the sequence that rose to the proportion of gross disobedience in the sight of God. Satan deceived Eve: Eve deceived Adam, or did she? Adam obeyed non the less and thereby bent away from God, an action that qualifies as man's first departure from the truth of his maker. To be sure, Adam had described his wife as "bone of my bone, and flesh of my flesh." (Gen. 2:23). So, he probably acted in error in honor of his love. However, here, we see a misplacement of trust. Adam, who should know better for his divine endowment, placed his faith on the lies of the Serpent and in honor of the bone of his bone and flesh of his flesh. He thus registered a zero value in the test of obedience. Apostle Paul was right when he recounted the creation model and maintained that Adam, being on a higher level, could not have been so deceived:

"But I suffer not a woman to usurp authority over the man...for Adam was first formed, then Eve. Adam was not deceived, but the woman being deceived was in the transgression" (1 Tim. 2:12-14).

Adam remains guilty of the sin of disobedience as the head of the woman and as the first parent of humanity. God did not curse the land on which the man would henceforth labor for food on the basis that Adam just disobeyed Him, but on the fact that he obeyed his wife instead of God:

"And unto Adam, he said, because thou hast hearkened unto the voice of thy wife, and hast eaten of the tree, of which I commanded thee, saying, Thou shalt not eat of it: Cursed is the ground for thy sake; in sorrow shalt, thou eat of it all the days of thy life" (Gen. 3:17).

Besides, knowledge is power. Before the Serpent's invitation, the first parents already knew about 'Goodness and Evil' inherent in the divine tree. What they lacked, therefore, was the exercise of trust in God. The Garden command comprised responsibilities that they failed to uphold but instead embraced the lure of lust. This reckless episode demonstrates man's inability to discern good and evil, truth and lie, a condition that immediately established human dependence on God, which is sustainable only through trust. Here, perhaps, is the most enduring result of the Fall of man. So, following the demise of innocence, man's nakedness and carnality were made bare. His directionless existence and the choice of struggle and labor would become a reality. Moreover, soon, he would begin to wander in the woods and toil for livelihood.

The man fell. Nevertheless, Jehovah God is all-merciful and all-caring; being touched by this act and knowing its impact on humanity, He sorted man out and asked the very first question of God to man: "Where art thou?" (Gen. 3:9). However, in the future, it would be the instance of the corrupted humanity to seek out God, the Redeemer:

"Where is he that is born King of the Jews?"(Mtt. 2:2). In the order of things of God, coincidence is not a variable. In the beginning, the Almighty God stretched out His hands to restore Humankind to Himself even when the first parents had carried out a damnable rebellion. However, man did not bend towards God but instead registered the first fruit of disobedience: Fear. Furthermore, the man went into hiding. Listen to Adam's response to the loaded query. Remarkably, in his revealed self-consciousness, the fallen man reacted in fear, not to God, but to the voice of God, a voice he had heard and cherished more than a thousand times in the past and a voice that had provided comfort as a soothing balm to his livelihood. However, on this occasion, Adam answered that same voice in anguish and fear:

"I heard thy voice in the garden, and I was afraid because I was naked, and I hid myself"(Gen. 3:10).

The corresponding words of God concerning the situation of the fallen man undermine every suggestion that we can explain away Adam's actions under the burdens of ignorance. How and why did Adam know that he was naked, and how did he conclude that the solution to his nakedness was "to hide"? Sin, if appreciated, will result in both shame and guilt, but repentance will always remain unanchored, without a subdued appreciation of the source of evil. We cannot turn around and walk away from corruption in such instances. Adam was aware of his stripped innocence but demonstrated a shying away from the sin itself. God in His merciful nature awakened him to this reality, but man advanced defenses and continued his inevitable descent down the slopes:

"The woman whom thou gavest to be with me, she gave me of the tree, and I did eat" (Gen 3:12).

Again, Eve countered:

"The Serpent beguiled me, and I did eat" (3:13). Perhaps this sequential transfer of guilt and responsibilities presents the genesis of self-justification. Denial of accountability occurs through the justification of related shortcomings. Unfortunately, this is why we experience delay in our expectations from the throne of mercy, because we routinely apply unguided available solutions to unacceptable behaviors.

However, God continues to inform us through symbols about his ordered salvation model in every situation. After the re-shape of the Adamic covenant, He made "coats of Animal Skins and clothed them" (Gen. 3:21). Earlier, Adam and Eve had covered their bodies with Figleaves, which probably left more than 90% of their bare bodies in glaring view of all. So, the product of their panic measure was inadequate both as material for clothing and a cover for shamefulness, nor was it appropriate to shield them from the guilt of disobedience and the inherent discomfort. The above scenario seems to paint a picture of salvation that must come from above, from God alone. It portrays redemption and divine covering for the soul of Humankind. Above all, it suggests a sacred painting of the absolute truth that man cannot hide from his sins or limitations, nor can he hide from God. The fig leaves adaption appears to instruct that those artificial solutions and freewill applications would not be a compliment in the order of the things of God. Nevertheless, there was a preceding judgment of curses on the soil on which Adam and humanity would henceforth labor for survival. Thus, Humankind began to toil for livelihood, as consequent of lust and pride (Gen. 3:17-18), and this has become the long-time effect of the Original Sin.

## MAN SINNED; MAN FELL, AND HE DIED.

The death of the man (Separation from God) is a result of sin. This eternal separation accompanies all unpleasantness which has become a lot of Humankind. Sin reigns, and because our first parents passed it down on humanity through the descendants of generations, all become soiled in iniquity:

"They are all gone out of the way, they are together become unprofitable; there is none that doeth good, no not one" (Rom. 2:12).

Moreover, all must die because of sin:

"And it is appointed unto men once to die, but after this the judgment" (Heb.9:27). Sin then is the direct cause of death. Nevertheless, what is sin, disobedience? The dictionary of Theology defines sin as "Anything contrary to the Law or will of God. For example, we have sinned if we lie because God has said not to lie (Exo.20:16). In addition, if you do not do what God has commanded (James 4:17), you sinned."

It would appear then that evil in the sight of God amounts to both commission and omission. The sin of the commission would suggest involvement in acts inconsistent with God's commands or human's outright foray into the actions that are repugnant to God's purity. The Laws of God—His dos and don'ts—conform to the very nature of God. This nature reflects His moral virtue, which man could only imagine than understand. His Law, then, must be composite of moral purity; and the reckless break away from the standards relative to this Law constitutes sin. There are also actions of omission relative to the commands of God. For instance, to neglect activities that would otherwise glorify God, regardless of the heights and depth or the persons therein, stand against moral standards and thus constitutes sin. Sin, therefore, is the transgression of the Law, command, or duty as set by God. Sin, whether by commission or omission, leads to bondage and death:

"For the wages of sin is death, but the gift of God is eternal life Jesus Christ our Lord" (Rom.6:23).

Thus, it has become that everyone lives under sin:

"What then? Are we better than they? No, in no way: for we have proved both Jews and Gentiles that they are all under sin." (Rom.3:9)

Furthermore, this maintains the painful separation of humanity from God of the universe. There is a bountiful presentation in the Scripture of the relationship between sin and death, as well as the fact that sin became Catholic (1 kg. 8:46; Eccl. 7:20; Rom. 3:23), having begun from Eden. The cursed ground and the thorns and thistles that the cursed land would henceforth bring are all death indices. Hitherto, and within the canopy of God, the man lacked nothing. Therefore, the toil and limitations that followed sin appear to be the instruments needed to instill humility unto humanity. Within this reality, pride will have to contend with grind and constraints to eliminate lust. The Preacher seems to be referring to this when he talks about "Travail" and the "Exercise" therein:

"For God giveth to a man that is good in his sight wisdom, knowledge, and joy: but to the sinner he giveth travail, to gather and heap up, that he may give to him that is good before God" (Eccl. 2:26).

Again, the Preacher says:

"I have seen the travail, which God hath given to the sons of men to be exercised in it." (Eccl.3:10). Sin lives in the similitude of clothing, tacitly woven upon man. It is an eternal replacement of the lost divine innocence. Because it is internally rooted in man, it effectively produces death only with a bit of nudge. For life to reign, man must put sin off his body and soul, but this can only happen under the canopy of divine leadership. Iniquity dominates the sphere of spiritual death. We can carve off this dominance only through repentance and obedience to God's words. It is no wonder that King Solomon, in advancing wisdom for "godly life in an ungodly world," intones:

"He that covereth his sins shall not prosper, but whoso confesses and forsakes them shall have mercy" (Prov. 28:13).

For the same reason that Jesus Christ, while illuminating the mind of his disciples regarding his coming death and resurrection, explains in no ambiguous terms the importance of teaching repentance and the remission of sins among all people of the earth. This directive was nothing short of a blanket invitation of every individual among all people for self-evaluation and a redress of the visible coats of sin (Lk.24:48).

## GOD HATES SIN

For proper comprehension of the level to which God places sin; and appreciation of the intensity with which He hates sin, it is expedient to pinpoint the characteristics of evil. Some scholars have expressed this point elsewhere that sin could not exist in the isolation of liberty and intelligence. These attributes of corruption appear to give a man his false confidence in sin nature, which lures him to believe that he is acting on the strength of independence and free will. Moral laws cannot operate in conditions devoid of free and voluntary choices because the respect and the will to behave within the borders of such rules must originate from within the mind. Law is therefore contiguous to liberty or free will. Arguably, this concept had existed before sin entered the earth. When God said, "Eat those fruits," but "Do not eat this fruit," the instruction seems to embody tacit freedom in the man and the will to choose. However, the first time he had the opportunity to exercise this freedom of choice at Eden, he exhibited the pitiful limitations of his free will, which earned him eternal unpleasantness.

Nevertheless, liberty and free will are unavoidable attributes of sin, constituting part of Adamic nature which all inherit through the bloodline. Regardless, when exercising the divine codes, arguments have no place. What is needed is listening and obedience. Again, sin operates in the confines of intelligence. We sin with full awareness of its wrongful nature because a law or command must exist for that effect for it to become a sin. God said, "Thou shall not kill" (Exo.20:13). This command becomes the parameter through which killing will qualify as sinful. In the absence of this law, there would not be any sin of murder, neither would a man be apprehensive about the act of killing, nor would the Word even exist in his consciousness. However, with the existing governing principle, anyone who kills would be doing so with the knowledge of the ruling moral code. Nevertheless, it is apt to reiterate that the holy book does not present any guideline for excluding the incomprehensible act of Sinning. Every one of the Adamic traits is a sinner:

"For all have sinned and come short of the glory of God" (Rom. 3:23). Therefore, we unnecessarily subject ourselves to the lure of academic excellence when we glorify the idea of knowledge, intelligence, and willpower as we consider the acts of Sinning. Whatever result emerges from such exercises must remain in the beauty of academic bubbles that change nothing in the spiritual realm.

All have sinned. Happily, there is nothing impossible with the Omniscient, whose ways are different from the ways of men. He made us all, and He knows us all. From the premise of His mercy, He informs us of our polluted essence with the pronouncement: "you have sinned." This declaration in no way suggests condemnation but a directive to re-focus our minds on purification to make us presentable before Him.

Perhaps a recount of God's reactions to wickedness will further illustrate the filthiness of sin in the eyes of God and the damaging nature of evil itself. Earlier, we saw that for the sinful nature of Humankind, a reasonable distance erupted to place a boundary between humans and the glory of God (Rom.3:23). God hates sin and regards the sinners as His enemies. Therefore, Adam and Eve earned expulsion from the garden because of one sin (Gen.3:23-24), just like Moses lost his privilege to lead the people of Israel into the Promised Land because of the sin at the waters of Meribah (Num.20:12-13). Gehazi also incurred the inglorious transfer of Naaman's leprosy, not only to his skin but to his descendants, for his actions of stealing (2Kg. 5:27). Similarly, Ananias and his wife met instant death for stealing from the Lord. (Acts 5:1-10).

Man cannot afford to be indifferent to sin because it immediately sustains our moral inadequacy and, before God, tables our filthiness. Still, the liberal mention in the Scripture of God's anger on those who sin should not suffice as the corrupt nature of God;

instead, it reflects His Holiness in reflex action against sin. Holiness and evil cannot cohabit, and being who he is, God's anger on sin and sinners appears instantaneous:

God is angry with the wicked every day." (Ps.7:11)

Again, the Psalmist advises:

"Serve the Lord with fear and rejoice with trembling. Kiss the Son lest he be angry, and you perish from the way when his wrath is kindled but a little."(Ps. 2:11-12)

God will render vengeance on his enemies and reward those who hate him. Therefore, enemies and those who hate him are the sinners:

"I will render vengeance to mine enemies and will reward them that hate me. I will make mine arrows drunk with blood, and my sword shall devour flesh; and that with the blood of the slain and of the captives from the beginning of revenge upon the enemy." (Deut.32:41-42).

<u>Some Instructing Verses on Sin.</u>

"Whosoever sinned also transgressed the law: for sin is the transgression of the law." (1 Jn.3:4)

"Then when lust hath conceived, it bringeth forth sin; and sin, when it is finished, bringeth forth death." (Jm. 1:11).

"Wherefore I say unto you, all manner of sin and blasphemy shall be forgiven unto men: but the blasphemy against the Holy Ghost shall not be forgiven unto men." (Mtt.12:31)

"Blessed is the man to whom the Lord will not impute sin." (Rom. 4:8)

"Therefore, to him, that knoweth to do good and doeth it not, it is a sin." (Jm.4:17)

"If we confess our sins, he is faithful and just to forgive us our sins and cleanse us from all unrighteousness." (1 Jn. 1:9)

"Whosoever abideth in him sinneth not: Whosoever sinneth hath not seen him, neither known him." (1 Jn. 3:6)

"Behold thou art made whole: sin no more, lest a worse thing come upon thee." (Jn.5:14)

## DEATH

This reality is the immediate result of sin. It suggests separation and/or the state of separation. Biblically, death presents two pictures. The first instance defines cessation of life, physical or spiritual. The second picture of death appears to hide in the fabrics of theology and academics.

Nevertheless, for its importance in the human relationship with God, it is one concept that we should reveal in the most straightforward language possible for all to grasp without hindrances. This death is the Life of Sin. It is a reference to eternal separation from God because of sin: "The Lord's hand is not shortened, that it cannot save; neither his ear heavy that it cannot hear: But your iniquities have separated between you and your God, and your sins have hid his face from you, that he will not hear" (Isa. 59:1-2).

This type is the incurred death by humanity's first parents through disobedience, a lawless exhibition of resentful behavior amid everything good. No matter, a law must receive a violation for sin to result in judgment, and the penalty is death, always: "For the wages of sin is Death" (Rom. 6:23). However, as death suggests a life of sin and thus a separation from God, it still refers to the cessation of life. We notice that the meaning of death continually betrays nothing short of the separation of one thing from the other. Physical death separates body and soul. The Preacher explains this experience exceedingly well with words woven around wisdom:

"Then shall the dust return to earth as it was: and the spirit shall return unto God who gave it" (Eccl.12:7).

We can also reason that the body separates from the soul from the words of Moses (Gen. 25:1), which James simplifies thus:

"For as the body without the spirit is dead, so faith without work is dead also" (James. 2:26). Therefore, we see that physical death cannot occur without the demise of the body. However, as proof of this occurrence and for the dust to return to Earth as it was, there is usually a traditional ceremony by the dead's people. In describing this,

Baker's Dictionary "sees death as mortality" and defines it as "The absence or withdrawal of breath and the life force that makes movement, metabolism, and interrelationship with others possible" (7).

On the other hand, spiritual death is different from physical death because we cannot see or touch it. It exists outside of the physical senses and suggests a state of being more than anything else. This death is the severance of man from God due to sin. In this realm, the man is a living dead: conscious of himself, fully aware of his existence, but oblivion of the power of God all around him. Although a walking spirit, he is spiritually blind, occasioned by the veil of iniquities. This man is physically strong and meets with tasks as applicable, but he is spiritually feeble, unrealized, and bounces with failures, especially with things divine. This separation was the type of death that Adam and Eve experienced in the Garden of Eden (Gen. 2:17), which Humankind inherited down the ages. It is the same kind of death that Ezekiel exposes while explaining that all souls belong to God, who would cause all such souls that sin to end:

"Behold, all souls are mine; as the soul of the father, so also the soul of the son is mine: the soul that sinneth, it shall die"(Eze.18:4).

We will agree that lifting this reference in the isolation of the chapter may bend it to present the meaning of the physical cessation of life: 'the soul is mine, and if the soul sins, I will take it.' However, the accompanying explanation, which climaxed in verse 9, denies this conclusion (Ezek. 18:5-8), and empowers the message: However, if the soul "Hath walked in my statutes, and hath kept my judgments, to deal truly; he is just, he shall surely live, saith the Lord God" (18:9).

The prophet then emphasized that the only solution to this dilemma was repentance and sinlessness (18:21). To instruct that the death he meant was not the physical cessation of life, he addressed the whole nation of Israel and appealed to them to endeavor not to die in sin. We can infer that the lives of every citizen of Israel could not extinguish, all at the same time, because of their sins. A different type of death must therefore imply:

"Cast away from you all your transgressions, whereby ye have transgressed, and make you a new heart and a new spirit: for why will ye die O house of Israel?" (Eze. 18:31). Again, our Lord Jesus, the Master, in the eloquent use of symbols and parables in explaining matters of Heaven and Earth to his listeners, used the word "dead" inclusively to distinguish between man's spiritual and physical demise. In that discourse about followership, he said to that disciple: "Follow me, and let the dead bury their dead." (MT. 8:22) The first "dead" suggests humanity full of iniquities, the living-dead, who are defiant and lawless, and in their shortsightedness and pride, are oblivion of the outstretched hands of salvation. Then, the picture of the second "dead" becomes clear. It refers to the physically dead father of that disciple, who here conjures a cessation of life.

We can deduce that Jesus Christ was saying, "follow me" if you will, but allow the spiritually dead to bury their physically dead counterpart: the living souls in God have nothing to do with the death of the separated from God. The Lord made this concept clearer in the Resurrection discourse, where he explained to Martha that anyone who believes in him would live again, their previous death nature, regardless. However, anyone who lives in him would never die—will not separate from him: "I am the resurrection, and the life: he that believeth in me, though he were dead, yet shall he live: And whosoever liveth and believeth in me shall never die" (Jn. 11:25).

Humanity viewed the concept of death and sin with profound seriousness which occasioned its significant presence in the Scripture. Before the common era, death appeared to be accepted with reverence and awe and sustained for a long time as an instrument of punishment for crimes viewed as heinous. In biblical times also, death was the ultimate sentence for severe crimes. Thus, death and matters of death were written about or mentioned up to 370 times in the Old Testament alone; with the plural, Deaths, appearing thrice: Jeremiah (16:4), Ezekiel (28:8), and (28:10); bringing the total number of times it is mentioned to 373 in the OT. Again, "Dead" appeared about 362 times. A simple summation will bring the impressive number of appearances in the OT to 735 times (8). We notice, too, that of the 39 books of the OT, only eight books are present with no record of 'Death' or 'Death' (Nehemiah, Daniel, Joel, Zachariah, Haggai, Zephaniah, Nahum, and Malachi).

Similarly, all the authors of the New Testament had liberal mentions of the concept. The issues of death appeared 22 times in Matthew's gospel; ten times in Mark, ten times in Luke, and 12 times in the gospel of John, equaling 54 times in the synoptic gospels. In the epistles, it appears about 82 times with the Theologian, Paul, championing the lead with about 56 times in instruction. The New Testament, therefore, presents 'death' 106 times. Thus, the teachings, dialogues, discourses, or otherwise on death issues appear about 841 times in the entire bible (8/2).

Nevertheless, because the issues of this concept captured the attention of biblical should not lead one to believe that they cherish human suffering. But it does suggest that death occupies a place of importance in bible messages because of sin. At the same time, it presents the undeniable truth of personified penalty for the most heinous acts of man during and before the Common Era. However, no matter how it comes, it occurs with the edge of finality, so sharp that it dazzles human imagination while bringing to fore the helplessness in the entire man to deal with the inevitable. The departed never comes back. Faced with this reality, King David decides to wine and dine at the death of his son:

"But now he is dead, wherefore should I fast? Can I bring him back? I shall go to him, but he shall not return to me." (11 Sam.12:23) David could not perform the feat of bringing back his son to life, and like every human, he did not even try to venture into that realm. Instead, he ate and drank in his wisdom and gave God the glory. Such is the finality of death, with no warning and no trace of choice. Nevertheless, we remain of the Lord, regardless:

"For whether we live, we live unto the Lord; and whether we die, we die unto the Lord: Whether we live therefore, or die, we are the Lord's." (Rom. 14:8)

However, to us as believers, it is expedient to die in the Lord so that we can rest, and our labor and our righteousness become our blessings: "Yea, saith the Spirit, that they may rest from their labors; and their works do follow them" (Rev. 14:13). True, reality insists that death (physical) is man's gateway from the earth's surface to the great beyond. Nevertheless, because it is employed to quicken this final chapter of man, it also exemplifies the seriousness of how God hates sin. When sin occurs, death happens. But, again, God does not qualify sin superlatively: There is no minor sin.

# CHAPTER TWO

## The Law of Sin and Death

It would appear then that death and sin are intertwined, inseparable even though incongruent. Without sin, death is nonexistent. Thus, while the sting of death is sin, the strength of corruption remains the Law (1 Cor.15:56). This reference suggests that the Law which the omniscient ordered in place to operate these two indestructible spirits has always been in the order of things. Paul observes that because "death reigned from Adam to Moses," everyone has become sinners, "for as by one man's disobedience many were made sinners" (Rom. 5:14-19).

To reign suggests a royal authority or an exercise of sovereign power or kingship. In such a manner, the personification of death seems a deliberate act to instill into the mind the strength and finality with which the monster operates. Apostle Paul, by the authority of the Holy Spirit, became aware of this Law. He became aware of his person and the knowledge of two individuals within him. He realized that he was not the one making most of his choices. Horrified that he had become captive to the Law of the Sin, which has many branches, he exclaimed: "O wretched man that I am! Who shall deliver me from the body of this death?" Then, continuing, he exclaimed with gratitude:

"I thank God through Jesus Christ our Lord. So then with the mind, I serve the Law of God; but with the flesh the Law of Sin" (Rom.7:25).

The above self-talk or profession outlines the climax of Paul's spiritual foray into his inner man, the analysis of his sinful acts, and the reasons thereof. His findings were astonishing, for he could now understand that it was through the flesh that the Law of Sin operates. However, his greatest joy seemed to be the revelation that Jesus Christ was the solution to the cyclic Tug-of-war instead of willpower or self-efforts. So then, Jesus Christ is the response that he received to solve the problem. However, what is this Law? How does it operate?

In the reasoning of Paul, unintentional sin manifests in him with each successive attempt to do good. This revealed knowledge translates into Law. The Law denies evil; neither is man per se evil. Moreover, when we examine it, its overriding initiative to promote goodness in humanity becomes apparent. Nevertheless, the Apostle noticed that his progressive willingness to do good successively bent him to accomplish evil acts. This corrupt leadership makes all his attempts to obey the Law abortive, and so, the zeal to do that which is right and follow the Law never produced obedience but rebellion.

Then, it dawned on him that this ruthless rebellion could not be coming out of him because of his good intentions. There must be something other than "self" that is responsible for the corruption. He reasoned that an entity distinct from him must be accountable for the evil manifestation. This other man was in him, but it was not him. Paul, therefore, was not evil; neither are men. The Apostle's overriding thought appears to rest on the premise of the flesh. He realized that whenever he employed willpower as an instrument to do right, it always resulted in the evil dispensation. So, the flesh presents as the condemned culprit.

Nevertheless, the entity within him rises to upturn the good intent unto evil manifestation each time he nudged the flesh to do good. Still, that entity is not suitable for him. Neither could he say that it is the flesh. Instead, this entity he identified as "sin":

"If then I do that which I would not, I consent unto the law that is good. Now then, it is no more I that do it, but Sin that dwelleth in me. For I know that in me (that is, in my flesh) dwelleth no good thing: for to will is present with me; but how to perform that which is good I find not."(Rom.7:16-18)

What stands impressive is that this other man, sin, never rises in isolation of constant stimuli, which is the vertical direction of the flesh to produce good acts. Arguably, this scenario sits like a picture of conspiracy between the entities to provide man the fillip towards death, for evil will always result in the separation of man from the divine. Be it as it may, it would amount to foolery for man to abandon the attempts to do good because that would inevitably invite the wrath of God. However, within its borders of reality, the perplexing situation has other options for accomplishing good deeds. Thus, having realized the hopelessness in the flesh and being evenly suspicious of the will-power, the Apostle cried out to God for help discerning the simple-complex situation. Intriguingly, he received an instant revelation from above, the death of Jesus Christ: "O wretched man that I am! Who shall deliver me from the body of this death? I thank God through Jesus Christ our Lord." (Rom.7:24-25)

Herein resides the answer. It is never in the flesh and most certainly not through the power of man. Instead, it is Jesus who saves and delivers man from sinful nature due to his accomplishments on the cross for those who will live in Christ: "And there is therefore now no condemnation to them which are in Christ Jesus, who walk not after the flesh, but after the Spirit. For the Law of the Spirit of life in Christ hath made free from the Law of Sin and death" (Rom.8:1-2). Therefore, this newfound Law in the Spirit of life in Christ is the singular solution to the governing Law of sin and death complexities. The inability of a man to challenge the subtle divide between sin and death was thus made bare. Today's man now has the necessary power to match the obstacles of sin and the attended claws of death.

Christ's death presents both as an atonement for the sins of many and seed to enable the harvest of man's soul unto salvation. This enshrined limitations in a man's ability to effectively bear on these challenges seem to originate from the Fall and thus posit Adam's inheritance. Therefore, Humankind has sin nature transmitted through the bloodline from the first parents.

However, let us bear in mind that Apostle Paul only discovered these Laws during a trip to the recesses of the divine sphere. Call it meditation or revelation, but the facts remain that whatever method he employed to arrive at the truths did not fall short of reason (Rom.7:13-25). He considered the conclusion evenly and reached it through an analysis of intertwined issues. They were truths not made manifest in the manner of the AHA moment. Notice that there is no record of Apostle Paul as a scientist; neither would he qualify, going by what we read of him, as an activist. On the contrary, his enduring life magnifies him as a man of God. An Apostle made as such from above and who, although did not enjoy the privilege of first-hand instruction from the Master like his peers, stood poles apart on admirable grounds.

Therefore, it stands to reason that his findings emerged from spiritual truths and that he spoke and wrote as made possible by the Holy Spirit. Nevertheless, his findings are truths, and they became laws because they were true. When understood, what 'IS' eventually becomes "Truth" because 'What Is' suggests existence. Understandably, such may only exist outside our conscious reality.

Arguably then, the Law of the Spirit of Life in Christ Jesus was alive amongst men before the era of Paul but unknown to many. In order words, we do not discover the truth because truth lives. This Law, although it has been in existence, became a revelation with the atonement of His blood: the lasting power of our cleansing. Again, at first impression, this Law of Sin and death (Rom. 8:2), seems to portray a reference to the Law of Moses, for these were the governing Laws for the chosen nation of Israel. Nevertheless, the epistle to the Romans contains a significant presence of the Mosaic Laws (Rom. 6:15; 7:1; 7:7), and how ineffective it had become in humanity's deliverance from the burden of sin.

True, Mosaic Laws are subjective to parallel punitive measures consequent on their violations, many of which incurred death. However, suggesting that these Laws encompass a burden to the people is questionable. At the same time, infer that Apostle Paul would surmise these Laws of Moses with "sin and death" would equal placing these Laws and the person of Moses under questionable characterization or adjudged as deadly and wicked. Thank God, for we know that Paul defended this Law with unmatched zeal and proclaimed that it was not the fault of this dilemma. The Law, he said, is not a sin, but it posits a compelling element in identifying sin: "What shall we say then? Is the Law sin? God forbid. Nay, I had not known sin, but by the Law: For I had not known lust, except the Law said, thou shall not covet" (Rom. 7:7). Apostle Paul then pronounces the Law as holy and pleasing:

"For sin taking occasion by the commandment, deceived me, and by it slew me. Wherefore, the Law is holy, and the commandment holy, and just and good." (Rom.7: 11-12).

Therefore, if the "Sin Nature" of man is evident in truth and stands as anything to go by; and if we accept the sin nature as originating from the Fall, then the Apostle was referring to the spoken words of Genesis 2:17; 3:7, and not the Mosaic Law as a whole: "But of the tree of knowledge of good and evil, thou shall not eat of it: for in the day that thou eatest thereof thou shall surely die" (Gen. 2:17).

The Death occurred in (Gen. 3:7), "And the eyes of them both were opened, and they knew that they were naked," and they proceeded to establish the beginning of man's self-effort by employing fig tree leaves as covering for their nakedness. Adamic curses and covenant followed (3:14-24), and then the separation of man from God became alive through expulsion from the garden (3:24). It would appear then that the Law of Sin and death has a logical string to Eden's experience and is not a Mosaic referent. It sounds more logical to relate the Garden of Eden experience to the Law of the Spirit of life in Christ Jesus because resurrection presents the only power against death. Resurrection defeats death, and this victory suffices in Jesus the Christ. We find that God spoke death into existence following disobedience and the lawlessness of carnal man. Through the atoning blood of His begotten Son, Jesus, cleansing was crowned and was made perfect via resurrection. Thus, we mock death:

"O death, where is thy string? O grave, where is thy victory?" (1 Cor. 15:55). We must understand that Jesus came, died, and was resurrected in vain if we think humanity can override sin nature by the power of self or Law or flesh: "I do not frustrate the grace of the Law: for if righteousness come by the Law, then Christ is dead in vain" (Gal.2: 21). Again, "Christ is become of no effect unto you, whosoever of you are justified by the Law; ye are fallen from Grace. For we through the Spirit wait for the hope of righteousness by faith" (Gal.5:4-5).

However, it would only be academic to comprehend this Law in the dimension of general principle within the human scheme of things. We know that Law occasions to sin. Without the Law, Sin would be non-existent. Arguably, Mosaic Law qualifies as occupying this general principle in human governance and occasioning sins in unimaginable numeric proportions. We have defined death as physical and spiritual separation from God due to corruption. However, Moses enacted his laws as instructed from above. They were God's laws and would occasion death if rebellion occurred against them.

The Law of Sin and death and the Law of the Spirit of life in Christ Jesus did not refer to Codes, Enactments, or Ordinances. Instead, they suggest divine "Truths" or principles governing authority and operating from the spiritual realm. For the former, God spoke it into being, and it matured into a trait for transmission down the generations of descendants of the first parent. This Law would have a dimmed picture of Mosaic referent from this perspective. And for the later, scriptural evidence exposes it as grace advanced to man through the cross experience.

## THE SIN NATURE

This concept is not the nature of sin, but the sin nature of humanity. This nature would imply the embodiment of man; his composition, which God spoke into his being following disobedience and Fall, and the subsequent loss of God's glory. Swaggart defines this as the bent of human beings toward sin (9), while Morris established that sin nature, although inherited from Adam and Eve just like death; man also incurred the tendencies to become sin. These tendencies had become so real and personal that man's sins have transgressed to the proportion of deliberate acts.

In other words, every man is responsible for his actions of sin because such acts are intentional and personal. True, the first parent may have bequeathed the Sinful Nature to generations down the ages. Still, the recklessness in disobeying moral standards is willful and in the parameter of freewill. Moreover, Sin Nature does not infer the acts of Sinning. There is the principle of sin, and there is the act of Sinning. The Sin Nature in this context would qualify as its principle, while the actions of Sinning would comprise what Apostle Paul enumerated in his epistle to the faithful in Corinth: "Know ye not that the unrighteous shall not inherit the kingdom of God? Be not deceived: neither fornicators, nor idolaters, nor effeminate, nor abusers of themselves with mankind, nor thieves, nor covetous, nor drunkards, nor revilers, nor extortioners, shall inherit the kingdom of God" (1 Cor. 6:9-10). To the Galatians, the Apostle also wrote with an expansion of these themes:

"Now the works of the flesh are manifest, which are Adultery, fornication, uncleanness, lasciviousness, idolatry, witchcraft, hatred, variance, emulations, wrath, strife, seditions, heresies, envying, murders, drunkenness, revellings, and such like..." (Gal. 5:19-21).

While these sins result from sinful nature, we can conclude that they are not the Sin Nature in themselves. Man has a Sin nature. It is no heresy to suggest that man has varied natures, with each operating from a spiritual realm different from the other. At the least, the Scripture affirms that man has a divine nature. God, by His divine powers, has given us all good things concerning life, including His divine nature: "Whereby are given unto us exceeding great and precious promises: that by these ye might be partakers of divine nature, having escaped the corruption that is in the world through lust." (11 Pet. 1:4)

This reference confirms that man has sin nature: "Knowing this, that our old man is crucified with him, that the body of sin might be destroyed, that henceforth we should not serve sin." (Rom. 6:6)

The above referent is a testimony that man's resurrected nature assumes leadership of the "New Man" after the body of sin has suffered destruction by the crucifixion of the "Old Man." This "old man" becomes a new creature because he died to sin. At this new birth, everything about him turns around and faces a new direction toward Christ Jesus:

"Therefore, if any man be in Christ, he is a new creature; old things are passed away; behold all things are become new." (11 Cor. 5:17)

However, in all these, there is a teasing dilemma. At the instant of the "Born again" experience, sin nature is only rendered ineffective and never extinguished. Therefore, the permanency of its attached strings to the human body makes it an implicit part of man. However, on the other hand, because of sin, it rises quickly to the surface and issues infallible directives that compel the body into obedience. For this reason, Apostle Paul advises:

"Let not sin therefore reign in your mortal body, that you should obey it in the lusts thereof. Neither yield you your members as instruments of unrighteousness unto sin: but yield yourselves unto God, as those who are alive from the dead, and your members as instruments of righteousness unto God" (Rom. 6:12-13). Nevertheless, we can emphasize that the power of this sin in man is not a result of unbelief of the Word, nor could it be said to be subject to ignorance of the redeeming power of the blood, nor the lack of faith thereof; instead, it emanates from the established order of things following the Fall. Consequently, it did not just become part of man, but it usurped kingship and established a monarchy in the carnal man. For this authority, therefore, the "sin nature" is liberally honored with terms like "Reign" (Rom.6:12) and "Dominion" (Rom.7:18). Thus, in one of his frustrating dialogues, Paul argues that because of the dominance of this overlord, he could not find the ability to perform good deeds:

"Now then, it is no more I that do it (commit sin), but sin that dwelleth in me. For I know that in me (in my flesh) dwelleth no good thing: for to will is present with me; but how to perform that which is good I find not" (Rom. 7:17-18).

The believer's life thrives in war and conflicts due to the desires of the flesh. Apostle James identifies this confusing continuum to his people in the diaspora, and explains that the wars and strife within their bodies originate from lust. This intent to please the flesh may well be why we continually fail to receive what we ask for, because we ask for a misplaced reason: the desires of the flesh. This human condition endures because there is another law in our member that pars against our mind. This other Law ultimately brings man to the subjection of the Law of Sin through the bidding of the flesh. The flesh then is the enemy, and the only weapon against this monster is the power of the Spirit. This flesh-enmity is why we must die in the flesh for the spirit-man to spring to leadership.

## HOW DID SIN-NATURE BECOME PART OF MAN?

The earth from the beginning received a divine structure to replenish by the efficacy of the seed principle:

"And God blessed them, and God said unto them, Be fruitful and multiply, and replenish the earth, and subdue it: and have dominion over...And God said, Behold I have given you every herb bearing seed, which is upon the face of all the earth, and every tree, in the which is the fruit of a tree yielding seed; to you, it shall be for meat." (Gen. 1:28-29)

The above is the seed principle upon which the beauty of the earth sustains renewal. We cannot question creation, but revival seems evident. We have also learned that understanding the visible world comes with comprehending the invisible truths. Jesus himself wove a comprehensive meaning of the seed principle for us, using a simple parable of a Sower. His hearers were agrarians which meant that the symbolism of a farmer made a perfect parallel. In this story, however, the planting and germination of a physical seed were used to unravel the varied dimensions inherent in the sowing of the Word of God.

The Lord thus employed the physical realities to espouse the hidden spiritual truth. Therefore, all truth is parallel; and, because of this eternal truth, there will always be 'planting,' and 'harvesting' and seasonal changes until the end of the earth: "While the earth remaineth seedtime and harvest, cold and heat, summer and winter, and day and night, shall not cease" (Gen. 8:22). The seedtime and harvest time represent the manifestation of governing principles that are indeed spiritual laws, hidden and unseen. Within this truth, we can see that the principle's dimensions are two: the physical and the spiritual. The former begets the latter; we discern the intangible and spiritual through the tangible and visible.

However, there is another reality within the spectrum of this spiritual realm: Faith. The farmer who sows maize, for instance, is faithful that maize will reproduce maize. His unshaken belief in the invisible we can call faith. To the extent that faith we employ on the plains of unwavering dedication in the things hoped for as inevitable, faith operates in the similitude of the seed principle. This stance agrees with the insight of the great Apostle: "Now, faith is the substance of things hoped for, the evidence of things not seen...through faith we understand that the worlds were framed by the word of God so that things which are seen were not made of things which do appear" (Heb. 11:1-3).

Faith then is a spiritual reality. Though naturally exploited for the present, it operates in the future, the sameness of the seed of thought. It captures the imagery of the product of belief, denying obstacles and oppositions. Instead, it harvests the expected outcomes in their completeness and delivers without defects. Faith denies uncertainties; neither is it a companion of the senses or a logic's complement. It rests squarely on the undiluted trust of the inner man of the divine. However, this does not militate against the fact that faith as a concept does grow from something. It develops from the seed sown according to its kind. The mustard seed's teaching paints a vivid picture of faith as seed: "And the Lord said, if ye had faith as a grain of mustard seed, ye might say unto this sycamore tree, Be thou plucked up by the root, and be thou planted in the sea: and it shall obey you" (Lk. 17:6).

Therefore, we should understand that faith must first begin as a seed and grow by its kind. Generally, for a seed to germinate through fruition, it needs good soil, time, and nurturing. This process suggests development. Thus, it is said: "Faith cometh by hearing and hearing by the word of God." (Rom.10:17). The belief-expectation produces its kind—the substance of "things hoped for." Therefore, faith grows in process and dimensions and as nurtured. Nevertheless, it anchors in the human Spirit. The same principle adheres to the reproduction of man. A sexual encounter implants the seed in a female in sperm, which germinates and develops into a new person. Just like a new plant contains the genetic codes transmitted from the parent seed, the genetic codes from the man transfer to the unique individual. Therefore, man-producing man will reproduce genetic sameness in the family tree through the bloodline and travel down descendants' generations. This hereditary transfer is a continuum. Should there be any more analysis to determine how the sin-nature of Adam, consequent of disobedience, became the portion of Humankind?

However, in the beginning, two kinds of seeds found expression in the mind of the first parents while they still lived in the Garden of Eden. First, it seems evident that Satan, the fallen Archangel (Isa. 14:12) sowed the seed of deception into man's mind, gaining entrance through the weaker sex, Eve. Second, his strength and subtleness for the success in this infamous act appeared to have found fillip from his likely position as the overseer of the Garden (Eze.8:13). This seed found fertile soil, as evident in the implied discontent with which Eve queried God's command. Unfortunately, by the time Adam told God they were hiding because they presented in nakedness, the seed had grown into fruitful proportions. Subsequently, Satan earns condemnation for his part in the process of this disobedience. However, the point of interest is not so much the curses bestowed on Satan, but the revelation of two seeds in the context: "I will put enmity between thee and the woman, and between thy seed and her seed; it shall bruise thy head, and thou shalt bruise his heel" (Gen. 3:15).

Notice that God did not ask the Serpent any question as He did other culprits. Instead, he administered judgment from His Omniscient. However, of utmost interest is the hidden message in the pronouncement, resting on "Thy seed and her seed" and "His heel." We notice that the woman's seed is suddenly qualified by a pronoun, "his," thereby revealing a picture of a man. The "seed of the woman" therefore transformed into a "he" instead of an "it." This qualification appears to project that God would undo what the Serpent had done to Humankind through its seed, and this found fulfillment in the seed of the virgin Mary. Her pregnancy was by the Word of God, for Mary had known no man.

In the dialogue that followed, we find that before the angel left her presence, Mary exercised an enviable belief and faith in the word of God. She traveled into the future and there harvested the fruit sowed by the Word of God: "Be it unto me according to thy word" (Lk. 1:38). Thus, Jesus, as the Word made flesh came and bruised Satan's head, unmade what he did, and delivered humanity from the shackles of sin. Therefore, Jesus Christ is the Logos, the Word of God, the creative order that became flesh and dwelt among men (Jn. 1:1-14). In agreement, Frank asserts: "The Logos is God in creation, revelation, and redemption" (10). Indeed, he is Light and Life.

We can now see the Sower's parable (Mk. 4:14ff) in its proper perspective. It presents the physical parallel in which the hidden truth lies to speed the understanding of the seed principle in the spiritual realm. However, one fact that we mostly omit in our understanding of the riddle is that the Sower's parable is the gateway to the mysteries of the Kingdom of God and the key to understanding all revealed knowledge. In their relaxed moment, the Apostles requested an explanation of the meaning of the parable, and he answered them and declared, "Unto you, it is given to know the mystery of the Kingdom of God: but unto them that are without, all these things are done in parables" (Mk. 4:11).

Jesus also asked them a question: "Know ye not this parable? And how then will you know all parables?" (4:13). The seed is the Word of God, and all hidden things and those kept in secret places must be revealed and brought to the open. The Word of God will always produce the fruits of the Spirit, which exemplifies a sparkling difference from the lies of the Serpent. These include love, joy, peace, longsuffering, gentleness, faith, meekness, and temperament. Because these are of the Spirit, they are exempt from the subjugation of any Law (Gal.5: 22-23).

# CHAPTER THREE

## The Mosaic Law

The awareness of "Moses" has become Catholic down the ages. It is a name with a liberal presence in the annals of history and an endearing persona in the journals of global religions. However, the name does not embody this colossal importance because of the miraculous scenarios surrounding his birth (Exo.2:1-10), nor because of his elevated status as the only prophet who knew and spoke with Yahweh face to face (Deut. 34:10), or because of his recorded excellence as a deliverer and nation-building, nor could it be because of the jaw-breaking miracles he performed beyond his time's realities (Exo. 8,9, 14:21-29).

Nevertheless, the mention of the name Moses does not immediately inspire admiration due to the efficiency of combining the offices of a Priest and Prophet. Instead, the inspiring essence of this name is the strength and beauty of the enduring Laws that he instituted (Deut. 5: 7-21), and which he nurtured to fruition. In cognizance of these Laws in Deuteronomy, Numbers, and Leviticus, his persona as a nation-builder dwarfs the line of historical and Biblical prophets since creation. Today, one is safe to state that the constitution and laws of the land, the attendant decrees, and punishments thereof of global democracies wear some Mosaic laws and ordinances. The Decalogue is mainly a point in issue. Within it, we find, "Thou shall not kill" (Exo.20:13), and "Thou shall not steal" (20:15). Although not stated precisely as such, these two laws and many others refuse denial in the moral Laws of most nations of the earth. Their enviable spot in the moral Laws of modern countries did not emanate from the way they sound or the character of their presentation, but because they exemplify undeniable truth and bear the core of moral responsibilities.

However, what are the Laws of Moses, and why did he give them? What part did these Laws play in man's redemption and relationship with God?  Easton, while analyzing mosaic laws, sees the code as instituted by Moses as: "The Laws of Moses is the whole body of Legislation (1kg. 2:3; 11kg 23:2; Ezra 3:2)." He sees the whole edict as basically theocratic and believes that these commandments of God present as the foundation of human duty (11). However, the Jews refer to the Law as Torah. This reference indicates the five books of Genesis, Exodus, Leviticus, Numbers, and Deuteronomy, which implies that the ordinances and enactments found in these books constitute The Law.

Nevertheless, even though 'Pentateuch,' 'Nomos,' and 'Torah' all refer to "five books," some Jewish Bible scholars deny Genesis inclusion in The Law. Emphatically, no apparent edict from whatever source appears to be present in the book of Genesis. Against this background, the Law would constitute only the instructive rituals, proclamations, and ordinances prescribed for the Israelites to enhance moral responsibilities. These Laws were fundamentally God's laws, but became Mosaic Laws because God enacted them through the instrumentality of Moses. The people heard it from him; he implemented them and monitored and nurtured them to the Laws of the land. Rightfully so, they were the Laws of Moses.

Some people tend to refer to the Mosaic Laws as the Ten Commandments only (Exo.20:1-17). This stance is hopeless because it suggests that the ten commandments present as the only reasonable Law of the land. Again, the ten-commandment referent denies the presence and usefulness of the ordinances and edicts running through the Torah. However, more importantly, it nullifies the general meaning of "The Law." Agreeable, therefore, the Law of Moses is both general and specific, intriguing and synergic, but unified under God. Amazingly, it envelopes and impacts every aspect of the human relationship with one another and with the Creator.

Thus, besides the Ten Commandments, The Law touches on the following aspects of human governance:

Moral Laws: e.g., murder/ordinances prescribed for the Israelites to enhance moral responsibilities. These Laws were fundamentally God's laws, but became Mosaic Laws because God enacted them through the instrumentality of Moses. The people heard it from him; he implemented them and monitored and nurtured them to the Laws of the land. Rightfully so, they were the Laws of Moses.

Food laws: clean and unclean foods/cooking and food storage.

Purity laws: e.g., on menstruation, seminal emissions/skin disease, and the like.

Feasts: Day of atonement/Passover/Feast of Tabernacles/Feast of unleavened bread/Feast of weeks.

Sacrifices and offerings: the sin offering/peace offering/drink offering/thanks offering/dough offering/scapegoat offering.

Instructions for the Priesthood and the High Priest, including tithes.

Instructions regarding the Tabernacle later applied to the Temple in Jerusalem, including those concerning the Holy of Holies containing the Ark of the Covenant and instructions for constructing many alters.

Forward-looking instructions for a time when Israel would demand a king.

Instructions for Proselytes and the Noahide (13).

We now know that the Old Testament law adds to about 613 commandments. Eminent scholars have identified and compiled these laws with their scriptural references (14) and sub-divided them into 248 positive mitzvoth and 365 negative mitzvoth, which adds up to 613 commandments. We find an example of mitzvoth about the blessing of God after meals in Deut. 8:10: "When thou hast eaten and art full, then thou shalt bless the Lord thy God for the good land which he hath given thee."

On Burnt Offerings, we notice the instruction: "And on a Sabbath day two lambs of the first year without spot, and two tenth deals of flour for a meat offering, mingled with oil, and the drink offering thereof" (Num.28:9).

Deuteronomy, Numbers, Exodus, and Leviticus are replete with similar dynamic instructions and ordinances enacted for the emerging Jewish societies. These Laws are unified in diversity, appearing in scattered oneness, but presenting as a family of codes unified under a common umbrella. Nevertheless, regardless of the complexities of the Law, evidence suggests that the Mosaic Law is powerful, compelling, and immediately binding to everyone. As a result, violators of the Law could earn themselves public execution (Deut.17:2-7). However, the glow of this Law presents coherence with successive covenants of God and the Hebrew Patriarchs, beginning with Abraham. Thus, the Mt Sinai law was in sequence with the Abrahamic covenant. Therefore, this Law was an arc of the continuum, positing divine furtherance of the plan for the restoration of God's chosen people. Thus, we read in 1Chr. 16:15-17:

"Be ye mindful always of this covenant; the word which he commanded to a thousand generations; Even of the covenant which he made with Abraham, and of his oath unto Isaac; And hath confirmed the same to Jacob for a law, and to Israel for an everlasting covenant."

It would also seem that the Law of Moses was meant for the consumption of the Israelites alone because Israel was the child of the promise. The Jerusalem Council (Acts. 15) under the Holy Spirit's auction decreed that non-Jews should not suffer discouragement with the forced observation of laws that never concerned them. This comforting news suggested to the Gentiles that the Jewish laws would remain within the confines of Jewish territories. Perhaps this singular release aided the speedy acceptance of the good news, because it put the social guard of divergent cultures at ease. Non-Jews were only required to abstain from meats offered to idols and from blood, fornication, and strangled animals. This spiritual gesture was a nudge of acceptance in isolation of cultural impositions.

Therefore, we can infer that Apostle Peter's missionary experience with Cornelius and his household was a precursor of the resolutions of the Jerusalem Council (Acts 10). Consequently, this household received the baptism of the Holy Spirit without the daunting presence of the Law. This feat confirmed that the old Law was not part of the new dispensation. For this soothing experience, Apostle Peter declared:

"Of a truth, I perceived that God is no respecter of persons. But in every nation, he who fears Him, and works righteousness, is accepted with Him" (Acts 10:34). Subsequently, Peter baptized this Gentile household in absolute disregard of the Law, because he witnessed that the men who knew no Law or ever heard of the Law received the outpouring of the Holy Spirit without the laying of hands.

The teaching was clear that there is no divide among men of all nations and that righteousness had emerged as the only variable for attaining salvation. It became clear that this salvation was not a birthright of the Jews, but universal for all peoples. From now on, the Apostles and every teacher of the Word were to "kill and eat" every creature for meat because they had been sanctified by God and purified by the blood of the Lamb of God. In all, because the non-Jews received the baptism of the Holy Spirit outside the confines of the Law, the invalidity of The Law in the current dispensation of Grace became apparent.

In retrospect, it is no wonder that Jesus, while still on Earth, presented many contrasts and deviations from the Law, especially concerning Sabbath traditions. He was continually and tacitly yelling out the limitations of the Law to his hearers while presenting the divine alternative. However, no one seemed articulate enough to discern any meaning from his instructive questionings and allegories, or everyone refused to embrace the truth of the matter. Thus, when the Pharisees challenged his acts which seemed inconsistent with the provision of the Law, Jesus countered with a question:

"Have you not read so much as this, what David did, when himself was hungry and they which were with him; how he went into the house of God and did take and eat the shewbread, and also gave to them that were with him; which it is not lawful to eat but for the priest alone?" (Lk. 6:3-4).

This reference to the actions of David in a moment of dire need (1Sam. 21:5-6) was an instructive masterpiece because David's exploits as a conqueror and distinguished leader of Israel presented a historical edifice cherished and admired by the people. Moreover, David, being who he was, understood the Law, and he was acquainted with the knowledge about the Shewbread. However, nevertheless, he ate the bread, gave some to his soldiers, and walked away unpunished. Under normal circumstances, even a priest who went into the Holy of Holies, which housed the bread in sinful robes, would have suffered an instant death, regardless of the Holy bread.

It would seem then that the circumstances of a genuine need, when presented in perspective, surpassed the provisions of the Law. A similar dissenting dialogue between Jesus and a Ruler of a Synagogue after he characteristically cured a woman of infirmity on a sabbath. The comparison between feeding an Ass on a Sabbath and healing a daughter of Abraham on the same day immediately revealed Christ's focus on Grace instead of the Law. With the contrasts between animals and men and the imagery of "Daughter of Abraham," he reminded everyone that the covenant was between God and Abraham, and not Abraham and domestic animals. Therefore, with these, Jesus insists that necessity denies recognition of the restraining claws of the Law:

"You hypocrite, does not each one of you on a Sabbath loose his ox or his ass from the stall and lead him away to watering? And ought not this woman, being a daughter of Abraham, whom Satan has bound, lo, these eighteen years, be loosed from the bound on a Sabbath Day?" (Lk. 6:15-16).

Meanwhile, what was the purpose of the Law? Why was it given? Did the Law live its usefulness, or was it an exercise in futility? Finally, what part did the Law play in the Socio-Political life of the Israelites? Irrespective of the Law's role as a guide for Israel towards a productive relationship with God, it seems persuasive that its divine purpose was to exhibit man's woeful inadequacies before him, and teach that man cannot redeem himself through the instrumentality of the Law. The Law's enormous character, and its diverse provision affecting every aspect of man, society, religion, and governance, made its observation unachievable for the man or for him to uphold unto righteousness. The identified 613 commandments of the Torah, plus moral Laws inherent in the Decalogue, seem to present a picture of a deliberate package of impossibilities before man. Who could obey all the Laws towards perfection? No mortal:

"For whosoever shall keep the whole Law, and yet offend in one point, he is guilty of all. For, he that said, do not commit adultery, also said, do not kill. Now, if you commit no adultery, yet if you kill, you have become a transgressor of the Law" (James. 2:10-11).

Therefore to the unruly and unrighteous people, such as Israel demonstrated from time to time, the Law offered a powerful administrative tool for a people, far more potent than a present-day constitution. Moreover, the Law reveals the nature of sin. Accordingly, we can state that the law was given only as a tool to define sin and not as the instrument to deliver man from the shackles of sin:

"Therefore, by the deeds of the Law there shall no flesh be justified in His sight: for by the Law is the knowledge revealed" (Rom. 3:20).

Interestingly, this same Law also declares man "guilty" before God (Rom. 3:19). We find that it unearthed sin out of the flesh, revealing and defining it. In the absence of a Law, we would not know evil. Sin becomes because the Law exists. Nevertheless, the Law could not save or deliver man and pronounce him guiltless. This scenario was humanity's tragic situation before something more than the Law emerged to save man and make everything anew.

However, it would seem that Moses, the greatest Lawgiver, enacted the Law as a standard of righteousness for God's chosen people. In one of many warning speeches during their desert experience, Moses asked the people:

"And what nation is there so great, that has Statutes and Judgments so righteous as all this Law, which I set before you this day?" (Deut.4:8) With such pronouncements, he was able to present the Law as the moral standard before the goodness and holiness of God. Therefore, holiness is imperative for the people because the Lord their God is holy, "the Commandment Holy, just and good" (Lev.19:2, Rom. 7:12).

One of the most endearing purposes of the Law is that which presents it as "a schoolmaster," "a teacher," and "a life guild" for the Jews:

"Wherefore, the Law was our schoolmaster, to bring us unto Christ, that we might be justified by faith." (Gal.3:24). Man could not make his own rules and draw out a self-enhanced plan for salvation; neither would it be appropriate for him to explore the futility of the flesh: will power, to bear goodness unto justification. We find, therefore, that although the law is holy and just, we see its strength only as a teacher, temporarily employed as a guild in transition until Christ and the New Covenant: "For Christ is the end of the Law for righteousness to everyone who believes" (Rom. 10:4).

However, within the fabrics of the Law, we find its tremendous impact on the religious-political life of God's people and its limitations as a guide and schoolmaster. This cherished guild could not eradicate sin nor enhance the desired relationship between man and his Creator, all because the Law was weak by the flesh. It became clear that man's desire for a brighter guide with the most potent beam sufficed to excite the lingering hindrances for humanity's emancipation and present man to God in an acceptable form. Therefore, Christ came so that Humankind would realize the righteousness of the Law in him (Rom.8:3). We also observe that the Law, by its very nature, denies faith, nor was it equipped to profess Grace. On the contrary, the heart of the Law is such that it only forces man to follow in line without any express divine presence, except the absence of punishment for not involving in the evil dispensation. Therefore, the great Apostle pronounced the Law as faithless, "And the Law is not of faith..." (Gal. 3:12).

If we compare the Law and this great Light in Christ Jesus viz-a-viz the relationship between man and God, or Earth and heavenly matters, we will find a handful of denials in the Law. First, the Law, in its weakness, could not make anything perfect, and for this reason, Paul states: "The law made nothing perfect...a better hope (in Christ Jesus) did." (Heb. 7:19). Instead, the Law only induced man into the abyss of limitless ordinances for which expectations man by his nature could not meet. Let us recall that the Torah contains about 613 directives in addition to the moral requirements in the original Ten Commandments. Is it not absurd to imagine it feasible for the man to observe these statutes in their completeness? Moreover, the Law seems to possess instruments of death and destruction within its claws while maintaining itself as the bondsman of sin. This stance agrees with what Paul advanced to the Romans:

"For I was alive without the Law once, but when the commandment came, sin revived, and I died. And the Commandment, which was ordained to life, I found to be unto death." (Rom. 7:9-10).

In other words, there is no victory for man by the validity of the Law. The Law does not save, nor does it contain the variables for justification within its beauty and power. The Law has no life. Therefore, neither could it lead humanity to righteousness. Nor can we say that the Law delivers man from iniquities through faith. Thus, the Law has nothing to do with deliverance, faith, and righteousness. The life experience of Father Abraham paints a picture of this reality. Let us recall that he earned righteousness through faith and belief in God without the intrigues of the Law: "And he believed in the Lord, and he counted it to him for righteousness" (Gen. 15:16). Faith, therefore, is identified as the primary requirement for righteousness. However, although truth insists that trust and obedience can procure righteousness, only in Christ Jesus could man fulfill the demands of the Law. Therefore, the Law itself teaches that man must look towards the Lamb of sacrifice for life eternal because no one is righteous except him:

"As it is written, there is non-righteous, no, not one" (Rom. 3:10).

Subsequently, "man is saved by grace through faith," and it is a gift of God (Eph. 3:10). So, even righteousness through works cannot justify, nor can man procure justification in the isolation of faith in Christ Jesus. Consequently, these are the dilemmas of the Law. Nevertheless, the Law did not strive in vain.

In the main, it stood out as a colossal revealer. In the absence of the Law, man could never have realized his corrupt nature and the reality of his filthiness. This state of enlightenment provided the fertile soil for the gospel to germinate. In achieving this, the Law presented as a balance of hope, for it instructed the people in the manner of redemption similitude of the coming Messiah. Enshrined in the maze of huddles inhibiting the observance of the Law was a system of balance that seems to suggest redemption exemplified in sacrifices and demonstrative offerings. The Lawgiver enacted these tenets to atone for the sins of all, and in these was the hope of anyone who sinned. Thus, we find the burnt offering, the peace offering, the sin offering, and the trespass offering under this tree of religion-traditional ceremonies.

In its wholeness, the Burnt offering (Lev. 1: 6; 6: 10-11), offers insight into the dept of sin rooted inside of a man. The ceremony of this offering depicts a symbolic transferring of sins upon the animal, an innocent culprit, just as the sinless Christ would carry the sins of humanity unto redemption. In the Peace offering (Lev.3), we also notice the symbolism of the Christ inducing peace by presenting man to God. The most apparent revelation here is the element of substitution for the offender's sins. Animals were used to substitute for the offender's sins (Lev. 3:2), just as Christ would die on man's behalf by becoming the substitution for his sins. Moreover, in the Sin-offering (Lev.4), we see Jesus typifying a "Sin Offering" for man. While the Trespass offering (Lev.5), was essentially cleanliness and purification. Therefore, we find that running through the harmonious ceremonies are four fundamental themes: sinning, atonement, substitution, and forgiveness. Although unexplained, the picture seemed to portray a symbolic demonstration of redemption through a perfect sacrifice in Christ Jesus. What could have become of Israel in the abyss of unattainable edicts without the atonement variables? Perhaps, this very mechanism exemplifies, more than anything else, the characteristics of the Law as a schoolteacher.

Nevertheless, we can infer that the Law also demonstrates the picture of love and Grace. Man's sinful nature could not provide him the fortitude to keep the Law or attain righteousness. Thus, the religious ceremonies offered immediate relief from disobedience. However, we can observe that the atonement and cleansing sacrifices present a continuum. It never ended. This exercise then was Grace, which offered to break the continuum's structure and free man from bondage. Therefore, it became pertinent to instruct and direct the peoples' minds to the coming Grace through Jesus Christ.

Meanwhile, Christ came to right the wrongs, fix the mess, and blot out the Law on man's behalf. While explaining this truth, Apostle Paul told the faithful at Colossi that Jesus' death had blotted "out the handwriting of ordinances that was against us, and took it out of the way, nailing it to the cross" (Col. 2:14). Finally, because the operation of the Law and its application exposed the limitations in the will of man, redeemed Israel, and the followers of Christ have an inevitable choice of a path to salvation. It is either "The Grace" or "The Law." It could never be both.

# CHAPTER FOUR

## The Law of The Spirit of Life in Christ Jesus

It is outside the realm of logic to conclude that it was through Adam that humanity harvested the infestation of sin and internal guilt. Therefore, Paul's apostolic discourse on this issue is Adamic referent. Man of a fact then was felled by disobedience and pride and earned the consequence of sin and its nature in which he thrives. Characteristically, the Apostle clarifies his message with an empowering contrast between judgment and condemnation on the one hand; and, on the other hand, righteousness and justification:

"Therefore, as by the offense of one judgment came upon all men to condemnation; even so by the righteousness of One the free gift came upon all men unto justification of life" (Rom. 5:18).

Thus, we find that humanity's condemnation for sin contrasts with the redeeming essence of Grace by Christ Jesus. Through one man's (Adam) offense, all became infested with internal guilt and rendered incapacitated by sinful nature. This infectious essence derails man's drive away from the direction of goodness. Man is sin, personified! Nevertheless, we also see a familiar pattern in the likeness of the cause as in the solution. Therefore, through the obedience of One man (Jesus), many are relieved of the effect of the original sin and made righteous by his Grace.  In this parallel, we can discern the Love and Goodness of God. The man brought curses and condemnation upon himself. He indulged himself in the invitation of eternal guilt with no external forces nudging him to action. Ultimately, a reckless choice within the confines of carnal wisdom became inevitable. Subsequently, humanity lost the instruction of the Omniscient. However, when Love emerged, the man had no contribution to the remedy but to open his mind and receive the gift of Grace. This analysis depicts the purity of His Highness, the God of creation.

However, we should not succumb to the visible temptation from the initial analysis. On the contrary, the synergy of Sin and Grace seems to present a picture of the inevitable foundation for Grace to reign unto righteousness. In other words, humanity must be soiled in iniquity to invite Grace. Nevertheless, Grace did not come to man because of the actions or activities of man. Instead, it is gifted, an unmerited hand-out to Humankind. It was this tempting analogy that prompted the great Apostle to advise the faithful in Rome:

"What shall we say then? Shall we continue to sin, that grace may abound? God forbid. How shall we, who are dead to sin, live any longer therein?" (Rom.6:1-2).

The contrast endures further. Man is made free from guilt and condemnation by our sojourn with Christ through baptism to death, and by trading our carnal strength for the guidance of the Holy Spirit, we receive new life through resurrection. Thus, Paul could rightly say, "There is therefore now no condemnation to them which are in Christ...for the Law of the Spirit in Christ Jesus has made me free from the Law of sin and death." (Rom.8: 1-2). It would appear then that the book of Romans chapter eight examines, in contrast, the essence between two of the most potent eternal principles in operation: **The Law of Sin and death; The Law of the Spirit of Life in Christ Jesus.** The former encases man in the limiting pentacles of separation and subjects him to the burden of sin. The latter, divinely willed, nullifies the efficacy of the former and pronounces man guiltless and justified in Christ. This acquittal presents the redeem with a clean slate of freedom. Consequently, there is no more judgment for the saved if he determines to thrive through belief and faith in Christ Jesus.

However, let us observe a quick clarification. We have suggested earlier that the Law of Sin and death referred to Eden's experience. Nevertheless, the "Law" here does not seem to indicate a referent to Genesis disobedience or the Law of Moses, or the Decalogue. Instead, this Law here is a principle, governing authority, and God-referent, and so is the Law of the Spirit in Christ Jesus. So then, we find a superlative inter-play of the triad laws. The school Teacher, which the Mosaic Law represents, prepared humanity for future realities. The Law of Sin and Death subject man to the burden of sin, while the Law of the Spirit of Life in Christ Jesus pronounces man guiltless and justified in Christ Jesus.

We also notice the forgiveness of sin and the power to override evil within this Law.

"There is, therefore, no condemnation to them which are in Christ..." (Rom.8:1), suggests forgiveness, especially for those who denounce self-will for the sake of Christ. However, "For the Law of the spirit of life in Christ Jesus has made me free from the Law of sin and death" (Rom.8:2), seems to suggest the power to override sin. Thus, given that man is incapable of defeating sin, this Law forgives and defeats sin on his behalf but goes further to crown him with authority to defeat evil. Therefore, man is first set free from the condemnation of sin and then enabled to subdue the "old man" in him.

Moreover, two other elements surface: baptism and sanctification. Finally, going a little backward in the Pauline epistle, we reference what might be the discourse that climaxed in Romans 8. Baptism unto Christ's death is the synchronizing element for forgiveness, justification, and sanctification. At the same time, it presents as a death blow to sin and condemnation: "Know you not that so many of us as were baptized into Jesus Christ were baptized into his death?" (Rom.6:3). Suppose our baptism implies a oneness with his death. In that case, it equally means that we experienced crucifixion and resurrection with him (Rom.6:6), and he that died and resurrected is free from sin. The meaning of all of this is remarkable. Man's condemnation by the Law is rendered null and void, with a resounding non-guilty verdict. This reality becomes because his baptism is into Christ's baptism, crucifixion, and resurrection. This baptism is the core of the mystery of the power that defeats evil and the Grace that forgives sin. Man is thus made perfect by the blood unto righteousness. Therefore, we can surmise that man by himself cannot defeat evil. Sin is forgiven only in Christ Jesus.

Nevertheless, we cannot forget the cross. The grace of the Holy Spirit did not find expression on Earth before the crucifixion, nor was the insistence of life in Christ as the solution to the flesh's dilemma. Therefore, we can assert that the Law of the Spirit of life in Christ Jesus anchors on the finished work of the cross. True, the prophets pre-warned about the coming Messiah, and John also taught about someone more significant than him who would baptize with fire. However, it is equally undeniable that the Lord Jesus did not carry out any act of baptism during his earthly ministry. After resurrection and ascension, we notice a dramatic departure from the baptism of repentance to a refreshing shift to the baptism unto his death with the outpouring of the Holy Spirit, just as he had promised in Acts 14:4-5.

The Pentecost stands as the turning point of this spiritual dimension, for it is there that the Apostles harvested the promise. The emersion of the Holy Spirit on the Apostles is a seed of empowerment, for subsequently, not only would they fearlessly preach Christ crucified, but the baptism of fire would through them manifest on anyone who believes. Therefore, we see Cornelius and his household receiving the same baptism of the Spirit as the Apostles, irrespective of their Gentile origin:

"While Peter yet spoke these words, the Holy Spirit fell on all of them which heard the words. And they of the circumcision which believed were astonished..." (Acts 10:44-45). This outpouring of the Holy Spirit at Pentecost signifies the beginning of a new era under his governance. Jesus Christ triumphed with his work on the cross and proclaimed the work as finished while he still hung there. The functioning power of the Holy Spirit flows from the divine realities of the cross, the realities of which the human mind may never fathom. This truth is why faith must be the deciding variable in the victory equation. Therefore, faith and the cross of Christ are the core substance of Christianity.

## THE CROSS

We find that the revelation of the cross relevance began in the distant past. The nullifying essence of the fiery Serpent as the cure for bite victims seems to present an acknowledgment of the redeeming power of the cross of Christ:

"...And the LORD said unto Moses, Make thee a fiery serpent, and set it upon a pole, and it shall come to pass, that everyone who is bitten when he looks upon it, shall live" (Num. 21: 6-8).

Many people had met their demise through the Serpent's bite. Those who survived only had to look up and cast their mind on the image of the fiery Serpent, which hung on a pole. This "lookup" exercise instantly produced one singular variable: Life. We know that this correlation is apt because Jesus confirmed the truth by referring to this desert experience and its relevance to him as the son of man. His dialogue with Nicodemus progressed to a point when he instructed his listeners with this revelation:

"And as Moses lifted up the serpent in the wilderness, even so, must the Son of Man be lifted up: That whosoever believes in Him should not perish but have Eternal Life" (Jn. 3:14-15). By the referent, we can recount that God the Father gave God the Son to the world, that through him, the world might inherit eternal life. In this experience, man needs only to believe in the Son to be relieved of condemnation of the Law. Jesus never came with a condemning agenda, but with saving grace and the justification of humanity in righteousness. Whether Nicodemus and other listeners understood the message is irrelevant at this point. It suffices that he sowed the seed.

Nevertheless, another truth persists from that referent. Jesus is the Messiah who would redeem man through death on the cross. Subsequently, just like the hung fiery Serpent of the desert experience, the cross would present as the symbol of divine essence upon which hangs humanity's victory against the condemnation of the Law of sin and death. Therefore, the cross of Christ is the anchor of the Law of the Spirit of life in Christ Jesus. It also posits the singular most essential index in God's redemptive plan. The cross stands on high grounds as the springboard of everything else: faith, purity, obedience, duty, profession, deliverance, and the governing Laws after Christ, which seem to revolve around it. Jesus the Christ received glorification at the end of this redemptive plan at the axis of the cross. Therefore, it cannot be over-emphasized that the believer's faith should build on the cross unto God for the tremendous journey of life.

Moreover, the potency of the cross appears to emanate from the finished work on the cross, which remains a mystery of the kingdom. If the world understood this mystery, they would not have hung the Son of Man. This truth, Paul reiterated to the faithful at Corinth: "But we speak the Wisdom of God in a mystery, even the hidden wisdom which God ordained before the world unto our glory: Which none of the princes of this world knew for had they known it, they would not have crucified the Lord of Glory" (1 Cor. 2:7-8). Nevertheless, what is this mystery? How did the cross come about, and what is this finished work on the cross? Then, again, how did it become the basis of the faith of every Christian?

The work of Christ on the cross comprised four phases of four dimensions and four precepts that denote rest. These precepts are Crucifixion, Descension, Resurrection, and Ascension.

**Crucifixion.** This phase of the work is the first dimension and first precept. It depicts the scourging, crucifixion, and subsequent death of Jesus. At this point, the mystery begins. The word unveils that we suffered crucifixion with Jesus, who died in the place of the sinful man so that he may destroy sin on behalf of humanity. In the same vein, since that Jesus rose from the dead, we also rose with him to the newness of life. Therefore, our "old man" with the embodied sinfulness stays crucified because we have become anew following the resurrection. This knowledge was the mystery that Apostle Paul unfolded when he wrote: "Knowing this, that our old man is crucified with Him, that the body of sin might be destroyed that henceforth we should not serve sin. For he who is dead is freed from sin. So now, if we are dead with Christ, we believe that we shall also live with him" (Rom. 6:6-8).

The crucifixion, therefore, epitomizes the substitutionary death of Jesus for the sake of humanity.

**Descension.** We are at the second phase of the finished work on the cross. This second phase describes the debt of the work and depicts Jesus' confrontation with the devil and the consequent stripping him of the powers with which he controlled man. Therefore, we can affirm that Jesus' death and his sojourn beneath the earth were not just traditional nor ceremonial. Instead, it was an ordained undertaking to fulfill his cause for humankind.

While examining this concept, Apostle John saw no difference between the devil and those who sin because the devil qualified as sin from the beginning. He informs us, therefore, that the purpose for which Jesus came was to destroy the works of the Devil: "He that committeth sin is of the devil; for the devil sinneth from the beginning. For this purpose, the Son of God was manifest, that he might destroy the works of the devil" (1Jn. 3:8). However, Apostle Paul explains that Christ fulfilled this purpose and accomplished the task at the cross. In one of his letters to the faithful at collates, he states: "And having spoiled principalities and powers, he made a show of them openly, triumphing over them in it" (Col.2:15).

**Resurrection.** This third phase of the work of love on the cross presents the third precept, the breadth, and the third dimension. At this junction, Jesus the Christ overpowered the grave, shamed death and its powers, and triumphantly rose unto life. With this accomplishment, he subdued all principalities and forces under his feet. Therefore, Christ will die no more, for death has no more dominion over him. Thus, Jesus' work on the cross was "a finished work." Nothing was left undone, and he did not reserve any task for the future. On the contrary, he nailed it and pronounced it "Finished."

Nevertheless, this work of love is for the benefit of humanity. When Christ died, we believe that we died with him. Therefore, now that he resurrects unto glory, we also know that we rose with him to the newness of life. Consequently, we are alive in God through Christ Jesus.

**Ascension.** This fourth phase is the height and the fourth dimension. It depicts his ride in glory into the Heavens far above the Earth and unto his preserved seat at the right hand of God, his Father.

This last phase was a glorious tower of a triumphant exit of the King of Kings, no doubt, to the remorse of the powers of the time. They would have realized the mistake of crucifying the Son of Man, because that singular undoing gave a fillip to the deliverance and justification of man. Then, the above analysis is the source of the CROSS, which Christ referred to when he was instructing his disciples on the most singular essential element they would need for effective discipleship: "If any man will come after me, let him deny himself, and take up his cross and follow me" (Mtt.16:24).

Nevertheless, let us bear in mind that Jesus is an unequal master in the use of allegory and parables to deliver his messages. Therefore, it is within the context of his character to employ his sacrificial symbol of the cross to teach his disciples what they must have to enable good followership in them. Although the physical crucifix suffices as the undeniable symbol of this sacrifice, Christ was instructively speaking about the denial of man's strength and ability in the flesh and the unconditional acceptance of the benefits of the finished works on the cross by Jesus the Christ. The above instruction suggests futility in work and duty if we follow Jesus without the cross and focus on "Christ Crucified."

Therefore, here is the mystery: Jesus completed the job on the cross, but we reap the benefit of this endurance by faith as sowed by the word of God. However, we do not harvest this benefit by good works, an excellent relationship with God, or keeping the commandments. Instead, it is the gift of God: "For by grace are you saved through faith, and not of yourself: it is the *gift of God; not of works, lest any man should boast" (Eph.2:8-9)*. Thus, we become a chosen generation, a royal priesthood, and a peculiar people because we are partakers of divine nature through Christ Jesus by his work on the cross. Here, he outwitted the prince of this world into crucifying him. The crucifixion was an unamendable mistake but a regrettable feat of the enemies. If they knew that Jesus was the invisible seed that would subject their kingdom to perpetual trauma, they would have ensured that no harm approached his person in the physical world (1Cor.2:7-8). Essentially, Christ outwitted the Devil on the cross. He failed to identify the eternal seed of Godhead, which the Lord God had nurtured to unmake the unpleasantness of the Law and undo the condemnation which she cast upon man. Therefore, because the Devil failed in his wisdom, he could not deny Christ the sacrifice on the cross, the ordained solution to humanity's dilemma.

In the end, Christ won, and because of this victory, we also won, having been washed in his blood unto justification. Society now emerges from the horrors of the Law as a condemned people, unto being a peculiar people and holy nation, chosen by God. This newness of life should be the source of our joy and the bone of our Christian exploits. We are complete in him and cleansed of all condemnations. It was a collective triumph that we are free from the law by the divine experience at calvary through Christ Jesus. Hitherto, death, the penalty of the law with its clogging craws, could not be atoned with animal's blood. Its atonement must be within the holiness of God alone, and for this cause, He ordained his son from the beginning.

This calvary experience thus paid the debt as conceived by God. But baptism immersed us into him to experience his death. This immersion incurs eternal finish that Jesus' death becomes our death. Subsequently, we are buried with him so that we can rise from the dead with him and similarly walk in the newness of life:

"Know you not that so many of us as were baptized into Jesus Christ were baptized into His Death? Therefore, we are buried with him by baptism into death: that like as Christ was raised up from the dead by the Glory of the Father, even so, we also should walk in newness of life" (Rom.6:3-5).

Henceforth, we become a new people, the treasure of God separated from all others. Therefore, it is expedient that we continually raise praises unto God almighty. Not only that he fulfilled his promise in making us chosen personas, but because in achieving this, we are relieved of our vacation in the darkness and brought into his shining presence. Meanwhile, we are free from the curse of the Law. However, we acknowledge that the law as it exists lacks the substance to separate man from the law of sin and death, nor was it enabled to induce eternal life, the focus of Christianity. This belief, by no means, suggests abhorrence to the commandments as issued by God. Nevertheless, it does lay bare the truth that although keeping the Law might qualify as a virtue, attempting to observe it without Christ is futile and fruitless.

In comfort, we observe that Christ is the anchor, and only through him can man uphold God's commandments for man's good. This parameter seems to echo the divine advice in John's gospel: "If you love me, keep my commandments" (Jn. 14:15).

Arguably, we can identify a delicate equilibrium between the law and grace. Although man could not keep the law as it exists, it undeniably occupies the apex of moral standards for peaceful coexistence. However, Jesus Christ as the anchor posits the means to that standard. The Law and the grace of God thus converge, tacitly, on the cross of Christ. Therefore, Jesus remains the way, the truth, and the life, and it is only through him could man reach the father in Heaven. Thus, Jesus is the means unto righteousness, and through him also, man assumes newness of life by his cross.

While maintaining the importance of the cross, Jesus reiterated that no one could even be his disciple in the absence of the cross: "And whosoever does not bear his cross, and come after me, cannot be my disciple" (Lk.14:27). It is only possible to become a joint heir with Christ through grace by the work on the cross. Healing comes from the cross; baptism of the Holy Spirit commenced after the cross; humanity's deliverance from the jaws of death is by the cross. Nor can we forget that at Calvary, Christ solved the problem of sin, for he is the Lamb who died in the place of the sinful man. Following this understanding, Apostle Paul vowed to emphasize only those things that concern Christ and his crucifixion: "I am determined not to know anything among you, save Jesus Christ and him crucified" (1Cor.2:2).

Subsequently, man becomes a new creature through the cross of Christ. Nevertheless, only the believer experiences this new life because he believes through faith in Christ Jesus. It would sound illogical, or at best, jaw-breaking oratory to suggest to an unbeliever that he was alive only because he died and rose from death with a man called Jesus. Faith thus suffices as the factor through which we pass and resurrect Christ unto the newness of life. The above analysis is why the principle and the exercise of faith will contend as the most singular potent principle in Christianity. We must conceive, execute, and harvest every desire from God by faith. Without trust, there is no

Christian- living, and we cannot access and make our request to God through Christ Jesus.

## THE LAW OF FAITH

"Where is boasting then? It is excluded. By what law? Of works? Nay: but by the Law of faith. Therefore, we conclude that a man is justified by faith without the deeds of the law" (Rom.3:27-28).

We receive justification by faith without the intrigues of the law. Jesus taught this principle of trust to his disciples and publicly declared through demonstrations in healing and deliverances the unparallel power of the faith principle. (Mt.6:30; Mk.10:52; Lk.12:28). However, its meaning and potency were never fully understood then as now. Yet, if we exclude faith from the equation of Christian life, what you have will be a colossal emptiness and helplessness. What is this Principle? How does it operate? From the scripture, we find that faith must begin as a seed. Cultivate it, and it will germinate and grow to fruition:

"If you have faith as a grain of mustard seed, you shall say unto this mountain, Remove hence to yonder place, and it shall remove." (Mt.17:20).

The idea of a seed inspires the imagination of cultivation. However, cultivating a seed does not happen overnight if this idea suffices. For one thing, it needs planting, watering, nurturing, harvesting, and replanting. Therefore, faith begins in belief as a seed, and it will grow and develop into a formidable tree unto fruition for harvesting. In this regard, the planting must be on fertile soil, which is the human mind. However, for another thing, the trust after activation must, through nurturing, grow to maturity. The method of achieving this is by hearing the word of God:

"So then, faith cometh by hearing, and hearing by the word of God." (Rom.10:17).

The primary way of hearing the word of God is by reading the scripture. The bible is the word of God written by the Holy Spirit through the instrumentality of chosen others. Therefore, a daily recourse to this living book nurtures your faith belief. Nevertheless, the world today has become a digital reality. The radio, television, and other broadcast media exist by which we can listen to the word of God. There are also numerous biblical magazines, books, booklets, and pamphlets by which one can experience the same effect. Yet, we cannot override the traditional pulpit renditions in churches and chapels alike. Therefore, for us Christians to share the full impact of faith, we must utilize these channels to nurture our beliefs daily. We should endeavor to exercise this because the Just must live by faith, being the righteousness of God. (Rom.1:17). Again, Jesus is the Word made flesh (Jn.1:14). In this cognizance, if we allow the Word to germinate in the spirit of man, it will produce the desirable Christian characteristics in the similitude of Christ.

The Word-made-flesh comprises the persona of Christ, his teachings, and his laws. When we imbibe these appropriately, we converge in his truth and persona and become Christ-like. Confidence and trust in him become a living reality in an uplifted consciousness. Faith becomes a reality within this realm of consciousness, a living substance inseparable from the Christian demeanor. In this reality, faith is an outright belief and trust in God without doubt and questioning. Therefore, it becomes the instrument of decrees and declarations, knowing that whatsoever desire we utter will receive an acknowledgment from the divine. We harvest in the belief, the substance of what we ask for, either now or in the future, even before encountering the substance of our desire. At this point, therefore, faith becomes "the substance of things hoped for, as well as the evidence of things not seen." (Heb.11:1).

Nevertheless, in as much as faith develops as a seed in man's mind, we are advised to be conscious of the source of mischief and filthiness and ensure that they do not mingle with the engrafted word of God.

(Jm.1:21). In other words, we must be conscious of the seeds we allow inside of us through the senses, for these would taint the word of God, the good seed. Therefore, whatever we allow ourselves to see, feel, imbibe through thoughts, and those words we release through the power of the tongue all constitute seeds. Consequently, all of these are the seeds being imposed on man by the enemy. Therefore, being aware of them and relentlessly walking away from them would endure the required constancy for complete victory in our faith run. Subsequently, ceaseless evangelism would find fertile soil to cultivate the good seed.

However, faith has a base. On what or whom should we exercise that undoubting belief in God? Jimmy Swaggart has an explanatory statement on the benefit of unwavering trust to the level that "God will pardon a sinner and forgive a believer based on that individual's exhibition of faith in Christ and what Christ did for us on the cross." (18). Therefore, God predicates His pardon and justification of sinners on the atoning sacrifice. Thus, the cross of Christ stands unchallenged as the basis of faith for Christ's followers. On the cross, he floored the Devil and won our glorious victory. Nevertheless, to realize the fullness of this cross-gifting on man, we must view the equation with keen interest. This process involves a consistent interaction between the Divine, Christ, the cross, and man. Thus, because the process denies complacency on the part of man, the redeem must focus on the journey of faith with unbending strength. Perhaps, this reasoning was why Jesus advised us in an unmistakable voice to abide in him, now that we are clean with the seed which he sowed in us:

"Abide in me, and I in you. As the branch cannot bear fruit of itself, except in the Vine; no more can you, except you abide in me" (Jn.15:4).

The imagery of a vine tree and its fruit-bearing branches paints a picture of the desired relationship between Christ and Christians. In line with this truth, any Christian detached from Jesus presents as a living-dead because Jesus Christ is the source of all nutrients that feed the branches. To understand the depth of the Lord's advice, let us explore the meaning of ABIDE. Regardless of all other interpretations, the sense in this context betrays "endurance without yielding" and "to bear patiently." It also suggests "stability" and "to remain in one place" (19). The above attributes of the branches of a vine are what the Lord is empowering us to possess. In the discourse, it is evident that choice was not available. Christ is the Vine, while the believers are the branches. Just as the vine branches could not produce fruits without the vine, Christians who disregard their attachments to Christ and his precepts lay fallow in their life exploits.

To further drive home the concept of steadfastness, Jesus characteristically continued with contrasting imageries. He had advised against reckless obedience to darkness or succumbing to the lure of the law (Jn.12:35,12:46), while succinctly affirming that he is the world's Light. As a redemption, you now have a choice between darkness, the Law, and Jesus, the Vine, and the Light. Let us also remember that later, he would reveal himself as "The way, the truth, and the Life." (Jn.14:6). We notice, therefore, the divine synergy of his persona for the redemption of humanity. The choice is self-explanatory. As the Light of the world, it is expedient that we walk in Jesus' footsteps to avoid pitfalls in darkness. But, as the truth, we must look up to him and the work on the cross to not abide in the lies of self-justification. Jesus is Life, at least for the faithful.

Therefore, we must see Christ as the unavoidable link in the redemptive process. Paul, the great Apostle, affirms that there is no more condemnation for those who believe in Christ. This gifting is because the Law of the Spirit of life in Christ Jesus obtained our freedom from the Law of Sin and Death. Thus, being in Christ anchors the basis for the benefits of our pardon and righteousness. It is the same oneness with him that empowers our authority over sin. In other words, our freedom from the condemnation of the Law rests on the complete work on the cross, where among other things, sin suffered condemnation in the flesh for us to stay clean in the flesh.

We are now in the spring of new life, leaving our former selves in the debris of old tradition in the distant past. With the soothing relief from the claws of the law comes the severance of the eternal struggle for justification. Henceforth, the guiltless believer ought to continually give God the glory not only that He instills in us the basis for our righteousness but because He first became our righteousness as a guiding Light.

## ACKNOWLEDGMENT

We have arrived at the stead of acknowledgment. To fully experience the benefits of the Law of the Spirit of life in Christ Jesus, we must become aware of our endowments following justification. However, this awareness will not find expression in our consciousness in isolation from the Word. We cannot unravel these hidden potentials in man in the absence of the knowledge of the word of God. The process must begin from what we know of the Word because we are renewed subsequently by the word of God. These good things are abundant and infinite if it is conceivable within man.

Nevertheless, we must acknowledge them by faith through Christ Jesus. (Philemon 6). The acknowledgment will occur through expression and profession, nonetheless. The word saves because the word is truth. The word renews the mind, and the word is Jesus, made flesh. Thus, Jesus assures the disciples that they are clean through the words he told them (Jn.15:3). Through the principle of acknowledgment of the new man, the power of sin is broken. Henceforth, the dominance of grace overrides the reign of sin. Therefore, the sovereignty of grace nullifies the claws of the law and its grip on humankind. Grace then springs man into a new life never yet imagined. Although it is expedient to present our bodies holy to be acceptable to God, it seems more rewarding to ooze such good righteousness on mind renewal. It is only on this platform could that prove the will of God.

We sustain our uniqueness in Christ Jesus through mind renewal, and the push to resist to exist in the similitude of the world becomes more dominant. Therefore, our transformation into newborns must be total and complete. In this regard, we must redo and rethink our ways to inspire others with our new selves. Thence, we become dead to sin, and because we live in this state of consciousness, we lose the feeling of sin, neither recognizing nor reacting to it. At this point, displacement must occur, for the human mind cannot be void. Our mixed reactions should now gear towards Christ because we live in him, and our actions in him must justify our just acquired death state. The belief in our completeness in Christ Jesus must find expression in our demeanor and accept all spiritual blessings that grace bestows on us. Justifiably, the kingdom of God is transformed within us in its perfect proportions through the work on the cross. Yet, it cannot find expression in the complacency of the inner man. It only enhances itself by applying the word of God, as exemplified in the seed principle. Therefore, we must first identify its existence in the spiritual realm and then speak it into reality in the physical with faith unto belief.

Subsequently, in exercising our faith, the Calvary should be the focal point, for it was here that the "old man" witnessed crucifixion with Him. Therefore, even if we must work, it must be in his belief by the injunction of the holy book:

"This is the work of God, that you believe on him whom He has sent" (Jn. 6:29).

The only remaining variable is the acceptance and conviction that we are dead to sin and freed from its web as proclaimed by the Lord: "It is finished."


## LIBERTY AS A LAW

Liberty is a principle we cannot overlook for the benefit of the new man. It is that authority to do the will of God within the confines of free will. Thus, within the word context, the believer has the freedom to live in the Peace of Christ as he will. He could decide to listen, imbibe, and do the work of God, or he could turn the other way round and follow the old tradition. The decision is on him and for him alone. This principle does not exist in the manner of "thou shall do this…" or "thou shall not do that…," but it presents as an unwritten companion of the divine pardon. It is the whole truth about the word of God.

While it is free and freely given, it is also the elastic glue between the bliss of Grace and the tentacles of the Law. The believer whose thought forms and exhibitions dangles within this elasticity has not experienced transformation through mind renewal.

Apostle James appears to be the first teacher to reference this principle. Admonishing the faithful, he writes:

"Whosoever looks into the perfect law of liberty and continues therein, he being not a forgetful hearer, but a doer of the work, this man shall be blessed in his deed" (James. 1:25). This advice seems to be a call not to rebel against the revealed truth of Christ, but instead to enhance the unimaginable blessings of God by obedience in doing the work of God.

Apostle Paul also referred to this principle while advising the new church in Galatia. He asked them to function within the provisions of this new law so as not to derail into the claws of the old law. "Stand fast therefore in the liberty wherewith Christ has made us free and be not entangled again with the yoke of bondage" (Gal.5:1ff). The ensuing discourse dangles contrasting choices between Christ and the Law. But, here again, we notice that man benefits nothing from the law.

Meanwhile, we are assured of victory when we focus our minds on Christ and internalize the cross as the object of our faith. Towards this truth, Jesus rests our minds with this declaration: "I am the way, the truth, and the life. No one comes to the Father but by me." (Jn. 14:6). The above is a revealed truth by the Word himself. If we desire the right path to walk on, Christ is that path. If we wish to find and uphold the reality of life, Christ is that truth. But if we aspire to seek and live in victory, then struggle no more, for Christ is life. With this precept, we will live blissfully in the father's presence by the unction of the Holy Spirit.

## THE LAW OF CHRIST

This almighty law seems apt at this junction because the negligence of its soothing balm would militate against the victory already won. But, on the other hand, the energy effortlessly incapacitates the arrows from the enemies of righteousness and the powers emanating from high places. This principle is *the Law of Love.* And it is probably for this understanding that the preacher taught: "Hatred stirreth up strifes: but love covereth all sins" (Prov. 10:12).

God is love, and anyone who does not have love in his heart could not possibly know God (1Jn.4:8). Moreover, He formed the earth in love and redeemed man in love. In this, the scripture agrees: "For God so loved the world that he gave his only begotten son, that whosoever believes in him should not perish, but have everlasting life" (Jn.3:16). It is unnecessary to define or explain what this love means or examine its texture and complexities. The holy scripture defines and describes the attributes of this love. The great Apostle Paul delved into this realm and wrote:

"Charity suffers long and is kind; charity envies not; Love vaunts not itself, is not puffed up, does not behave itself unseemly, seeks not her own, is not easily provoked, thinks no evil; Rejoices not in iniquity, but rejoices in the truth; bears all things, believes all things, endures all things" (1Cor.13:4-7). Here, we find the characteristics in the meaning of Love (Charity). First, it operates in the realm of patience, and its embodied kindness is the divine attribute of care. Second, love is emotionally and physically contended and does not cherish the belongings of others. Third, this essence is neither boastful nor arrogant, yet it is devoid of pride. It rejoices in truth only and cannot succumb to anger. Finally, love is an essence so natural and so divine that failure cannot stand near its tent.

Thus, we find that love stands unmovable as a glittering rock, oozing out tenderness and attracting everything good for peaceful co-existence. **Love then is the law of Christ,** which we are supposed to employ continually to nourish ourselves and then, for the service of humanity. It is also on the premise of this charity that we cannot judge our neighbors. Instead, the power of love should be the ready resource to energize and redirect our failing members towards the cross or encourage and guide them unto righteousness. It should not be far-fetched to understand Paul's position when he wrote: "For that which I do I allow: for what I would, that I do not; but what I hate, that I do" (Rom.7:15). This passage exemplifies the fact that we have all found ourselves within the perimeters of such helplessness at one point in our lives. Therefore, when we see our neighbor struggling in the web of trials, the response must never be the attitude of condemnation but rather applying the tenets of love to soothe the wounds, wipe the tears, and steer the wheel. Living with this consciousness of care would mean loving your neighbor as yourself, and when you love, you fulfill the law:

"Owe no man anything, but to love one another: for he that loves another has fulfilled the law" (Rom.13:8).

It is very instructive that almost every epistle to the early churches and new converts alike received the instruction to exercise this law of love. It is doubtful that the church would have survived without obedience to this instruction. Love indeed is a nullifying essence within self and among one another. Imputing this in our service to humankind, Peter echoes: "Beloved, let us love one another: for love is God, and everyone who loves is born of God and knows God" (1Jn.4:7). Paul also writes, "Brethren, you have been called unto liberty; only use not liberty for an occasion to the flesh, but by love serve one another" (Gal.5:13).

In other words, must we use our liberty or the newly auctioned freedom by the work on the cross to serve "self"? To relent in this would be a turnaround to carnal wisdom and a return to the old tradition of darkness. So instead, we are to exhibit love continually to enhance the bliss in justification through Christ Jesus.

Therefore, we notice that the freedom we gained from the Law and our gift of power over sin, our justification, and sanctification are not self-efforts or willpower earnings. So again, it is not from the corridors of great learning and carnal intelligence. These are giftings from the Love of God. Christ came to us by this Love in which he also bore our pains and embraced our death that we may live. This substitutionary exchange was the reason for which he came, to condemn sin in the flesh and deliver man from the inherent entanglement: "For what the law could not do in that it was weak through the flesh, God sending His own Son in the likeness of sinful flesh, and for sin, condemned sin in the flesh" (Rom.8:3).

We find in all these the comforting truth that loving God, in turn, gives strength, for God is LOVE. There should also be no argument that there would not be anything called Christianity without Jesus Christ and his glorified work on the cross. Let us remember that man's redemption came about in the stead of this same cross. Within these premises, we would not be out of tune to epitomize the themes of the Bible as the redemption of man in Christ Jesus and the end of the Law. Therefore, by his instructions, we must pick up our crosses daily and walk after him if we so desire to access the holy of holies.

Our object of faith should be the cross of Christ and him crucified. This revelation is why the claim of justification from the body of sin and sanctification unto victory remains by faith in Christ Jesus: "Therefore, being justified by faith, we have the peace with God through our Lord Jesus Christ" (Rom.5:1).

Nevertheless, to gain stability in this faith journey, we must always strive within the realities of our inabilities to exhibit our good intentions. In this reality, the importance of Divine Guidance becomes apparent. By his feeble self, the man cannot override the powers that push him away from the course of righteousness. Thus, man's self-efforts, willpower, observance of the law, and works, are unacceptable variables in the stride towards victorious living. Thankfully, the potent

Law which nullifies every other militating principle against our psyche is now available on the platter of gold. This directive is the law of the spirit of life in Christ Jesus. (Rom.8:2). This Law is reigning, for it has extinguished the condemnation from the bodies and midst of those in Christ Jesus.

# NOTES


1. *Harrison, Everett, ed., Baker's Dictionary of Theology, Grand Rapids: Baker Book House, 1960. Page 488.*
2. *Easton's Bible Dictionary, 18187: Biblegateway.com/Dictionary. Accessed 11/12/13.*
3. *The Genesis Records. Henry M. Morris, 2009. Page 110,113.*
4. *Smith's Bible Dictionary. Accessed 11/12/13.*
5. *The Expositor's Study Bible. King James Version. Giant Print Edition, Jimmy Swaggart, 2010. Page 1863.*
6. *The Genesis Record. Henry Morris, 2009. Page 110.*
7. *Baker's Evangelical Dictionary of Bible Theology.*
8. *The New Strong's Exhaustive Concordance of the Bible. Thomas Nelson Publishers, 2010. Page 209-301. Also, 8-2*
9. *The Sin Nature: A Study Guide. Published by Jimmy Swaggart, World Evangelism Press, page 35.*
10. *Frank Stagg: New Testament Theology. Broadman, 1962. ISBN: 978-0-8054-1613-8*
11. *Law of Moses: Easton's 1897 Bible Dictionary, 05, Jan 2014.Dictionary.com: http://dictionary.reference.com/browse/law of Moses.*
12. *Xxxxxxxxxxxxxxx.*
13. *Lifted from Wikipedia, the free encyclopedia:*

*http://wikipedia.org/wiki/law of Moses.*

14. *See work on 613 Mosaic Laws: http://gods-word-first.org/bible-study/613 commandments. Also, 613 commandments: http://en.wikipedia.org/wiki/613-mitzvot.*

15. *xxxxxxxxxxxx.*

16. *Charles Hodge(1797-1898); Quoted by grace to you at: http://www.gty.org.*

17. *See lecture notes of The Sure Foundation Theological Institute: The Seed Principle: http://www.theologicalinstitute.com/Video/seedText.html.*

18. *The Law of Spirit: A Study Guide. Published by Jimmy Swaggart, World Evangelism Press, Louisiana, 2008. Page 53.*

19. *Collegiate Dictionary; Merriam Webster, tenth Edition. Merriam-Webster, Incorporated, 191094.*

20. *See lecture notes of The Sure Foundation Theological Institute: The mind is the battle Ground: http://www.theologicalinstitute.com/Video/seedText.html.*

# REFERENCES


Borgman, Paul: *David, Saul, and God; Rediscovering an Ancient Story.* Oxford University Press, 2008.ISBN: 9780195331608.

Dictionary of Theology: *http://www.carm.org/dictionary/theology.*

Douglas, Moo. S: *The Epistle to the Romans: New International Commentary on the New Testament (NICNT), WM. B& Erdmann's publishing co., 1996.*

Geiser, ed; *Baker Encyclopedia of Christian Apologetics. Grand Rapids, M.I. Baker Book House, 2000.*

Gerhard Von Rad: *Old Testament Theology, Volume 1. The theology of Israel's Historical Traditions, Westminster John Knox Press, 2001. ISBN: 0-664-22407-5.*

Gerhard Von Rad: *Old Testament theology volume 2. The theology of Israel's Prophetic Traditions; Westminster John Knox Press, 2001. ISBN: 0-664-22408-3.*

*Grudem, Wayne: Systemic Theology. Grand Rapids, M.I Zondervan Publishing House, 1994.*

*Henry Morris: The Genesis Record: A scientific and devotional commentary on the Book of Beginnings. Baker Books, 2009. ISBN: 13:978-0801072826.*

*Jimmy Swaggart: The seventh chapter of Romans: A Study Guide. World Evangelism Press, Baton Rouge, Louisiana, 2008. ISBN: 978-1-934655-41-2.*

*Jimmy Swaggart: The Law of the Spirit: A Study Guide. World Evangelism Press, Baton Rouge, Louisiana, 2006. ISBN: 978-1934655-26-0.*

*Jimmy Swaggart: The Sin Nature: A Study Guide. World Evangelism Press, Baton Rouge, Louisiana, 2005. ISBN: 978-1-934655-27-6.*

*Kugel, James: traditions of the Bible: A guide to the Bible as it was at the start of the Common Era. Mass. Harvard University Press. ISBN: 9780674791510.*

*Law of Moses: Easton's 1847 Bible Dictionary, 05 Jan. 2004. Dictionary.com: http://dictionaary.reference.com/browse/law of Moses.*

*Merriam, Webster: Collegiate Dictionary, Tenth Edition, Merriam-Webster Incorporated, 1994. ISBN: 0-87779-709-9.*

*The American Heritage Dictionary of English Language, 4th edition, published by Houghton Mifflin.*

*The Holy Bible, Old and New Testaments; Authorized King James Version. Thomas Nelson Incorporated, Columbia, 2003.*

*The New Strong's Exhaustive Concordance of the Bible.* Thomas Nelson Publishers, 2010. ISBN: 978-1-4185-4169-9.

*Udo Schnelle: Theology of the New Testament; translated by Eugene Boring. Baker Publishing Group, Grand Rapids, 2009.*